Performance Disputes in Shipping

A Collection of Case Notes from India

Performance Disputes in Shipping

A Collection of Case Notes from India

Mayank Suri

Copyright © Mayank Suri, 2024

All rights reserved. No part of this publication may be reproduced, stored in a retrieval system, or transmitted in any form or by any means, electronic, mechanical, recording or otherwise, without the prior written permission of the author.

This book has been published with all efforts taken to make the material error-free after the consent of the author. However, the author and the publisher do not assume and hereby disclaim any liability to any party for any loss, damage, or disruption caused by errors or omissions, whether such errors or omissions result from negligence, accident, or any other cause. In addition, the author and the publisher do not represent or warrant that the information accessible via this book is accurate, complete or current.

Paperback ISBN: 979-8-89171-107-5

eBook ISBN: 979-8-89171-108-2

First Published in August, 2024

Published by Walnut Academia

(an imprint of Vyusta Ventures LLP)

www.walnutacademia.com

India

Unit# 909, 9th Floor, Wave Silver Tower, Sector-18, Noida - 201301

USA

1820 Avenue M #849, Brooklyn, NY 11230, United States of America

Distributed by

To students everywhere,

Like the class of LLB 2022 (Section C) at Jindal Global Law School

Acknowledgment

Maritime law, or the law of ships and cargo, is treated as a niche in the legal world. One of my aims has been to make its knowledge more accessible and easily understood. This work in synthesis reflects that aim.

It all started on the drawing board working with Captain Pankaj Mishra in the fall of 2022 in London. I was proposing to him some business ideas and at that time the idea of a compendium on Indian shipping cases came about. I was returning to India after a year in Singapore and was about to teach the law of contract to another batch of students. It was by instinct that I proposed the idea of this compendium to my class, LLB 2022 (Section C) at Jindal Global Law School. Shipping provides a fertile field for the study of contracts as this book will testify. Initially, 57 students, for reasons of necessity and enterprise, went about searching for cases from India, Hong Kong, and Singapore, relating to performance disputes based on a specific shipping contract, the charterparty. Identifying that judgments from India required the most visibility, 40 Indian judgments have found their way into this work.

I have attempted to explain the main point of dispute in each of the judgments in the simplest and clearest way possible. However, no one is above making mistakes and I hope that if any mistakes are found I am forgiven for making them.

Every work is a result of participation of several people. I am grateful to my three research assistants who joined me in the later stages of this work to recheck and attest to its readability: Sudeshna Sahu, Gaurie Mehra, and Khushi. There is a lot of promise in these three.

My experiences of maritime law and industry have informed the thought that led to this project and therefore, many people deserve recognition. These include my professors at Swansea University who taught me the subject, to the many friends I made there who are now in the professional thick of the global maritime and legal business, and the people I have worked with.

Finally, to friends and family, who have little idea of what I do daily but stand by me, nonetheless.

Mayank Suri

19th May 2024

Contents

Introduction 1

Mainly Relating to Ship 4

    Redelivery Default, Expired Charterparty, Agreement by Conduct . 5

        1.   Title: Bharat Petroleum Corporation Ltd *versus* Great Eastern Shipping Co Ltd 5

    Incompatible Port, Laytime, Responsibility 7

        2.   Title: Shipping Corporation of India Ltd *versus* Mare Shipping Inc 7

    Dispossession of Ship, Omitted Lay Days, Reasonability 10

        3.   Title: Andrew Yule and Co *versus* Ardeshir Bomanji Dubash 10

    Engine Breakdown, Laytime Calculation, Scope of Clause 12

        4.   Title: Steel Authority of India Ltd *versus* Pacific Gulf Shipping Co Ltd 12

    Dysfunctional Equipment, Validity of NoR, Specified Consequences 14

        5.   Title: Steel Authority of India (SAIL) *versus* Dampskibaselsbaket Norden 14

    Withdrawal of Ship, Hire Payment Deductions, Possessory Rights 18

        6.   Title: Indian Oil Corporation Ltd *versus* Thakur Shipping Co Ltd 18

    Cancellation of Carriage, Concluded Contract, Express Terms and Intention 21

        7.   Title: Trimex International FZE Ltd Dubai *versus* Vedanta Aluminium Ltd India 21

v

Expiry of Term of Performance, Laycan, Reasonability 24

    8. Title: Steel Authority of India Ltd *versus* Jaldhi Overseas Pte Ltd 24

Frustrated Charterparty, Advance Freight, Domestic Law 27

    9. Title: Gandha Korliah *versus* Janoo Hassan 27

Delivery Default, Role of Disponent Owner, Remedy 29

    10. Title: Epoch Enterrepots *versus* MV Won Fu 29

Draft Charterparty, Condition to Formation, Intention 31

    11. Title: Rickmers Verwaltung GmbH *versus* Indian Oil Corporation Ltd 31

Redelivery Default, Off Hire Clause, Ordinary Meaning 34

    12. Title: Wizdoms Naik International Limited *versus* DSV Gerimal (IMO No 7932240) 34

Delay, Risk Allocation, Contract Terms 37

    13. Title: Bridge Marine Ltd *versus* Indian Oil Corporation Limited 37

Refusal to Load, Disponent Owner, Admiralty Jurisdiction 41

    14. Title: MV Leonis *versus* Libra Shipping Services LLC 41

Failure to Mobilise, Bank Guarantee, Separability 43

    15. Title: Rolv Berg Drive A/S *versus* Oil and Natural Gas Corporation Ltd 43

Mainly Relating to Cargo 46

Slack Bags, Unknown Weight, Burden of Proof 47

    16. Title: Thakur Shipping Co Ltd Bombay *versus* Food Corporation of India 47

Shortage of Goods Received, Discharge Clauses, Pragmatic Interpretation 50

    17. Title: General Traders Ltd *versus* Pierce Leslie (India) Ltd.. 50

Damaged Cargo, Role of Inspection, Material Difference 53

    18. Title: SGS India Ltd *versus* Dolphin International Ltd 53

Wrong Goods, Nature Unknown, Non-Admiralty Breach 55

    19. Title: National Co Ltd *versus* MS Asia Mariner 55

Damaged Cargo, Incorporation Clause, Intent 58

    20. Title: MV Baltic Confidence *versus* State of Trading Corporation of India Ltd 58

Rejected Goods, Agent's Negligence, Frustration of Remedy 60

    21. Title: Penguin Maritime Ltd *versus* Lee & Muirhead Ltd 60

Shortage and Damage to Goods Received, Clean Bill of Lading, Balance of Evidence 63

    22. Title: Jayanti Shipping Co Ltd *versus* The Food Corporation of India 63

Shortage of Goods Received, Unattended Arbitration Notice, Effect of Silence and Inaction 66

    23. Title: Food Corporation of India *versus* Thakur Shipping Co 66

Rejected Goods, Deviation, Intervening Acts 69

    24. Title: Priyanka Overseas Pvt Ltd *versus* Joongang Shipping Co Ltd 69

Delayed Delivery, Foreseeable Losses, Information 71

    25. Title: MV Quang Minh 126 *versus* Bohra Industries Ltd 71

Damaged Goods, Applicable Law, Intent 74

    26. Title: Indian Shipping Industry Ltd *versus* Dominion of India 74

Misdelivery, Bills of Lading, Agent's Responsibility 77

    27. Title: Shaw Wallace & Co Ltd *versus* Nepal Food Corporation 77

Mainly Relating to Documents 81

Demurrage, Nature of Clause, Intention and Understanding 82

    28. Title: Ultratech Cement Ltd *versus* Sunfield Resources Pty Ltd 82

Charterparty Repudiation, Broker's Letter of Guarantee, Knowledge of Obligation 85

    29. Title: POL India Projects Ltd *versus* Aurelia Reederei Eugen Friederich GmbH Schiffahrtsgesellschaft & Company KG. 85

Bunker Payment, Privity, Terms and Conduct 88

    30. Title: Chemoil Adani Pvt Ltd *versus* MV Hansa Sonderburg 88

Demurrage, Exception of Restraints of Established Authorities, Effect of 'Without Fault' 91

    31. Title: MMTC of India Ltd *versus* Interore Fertichem Resources SA 91

Calculation of Laytime 94

    32. Title: Jayshree Shipping *versus* Food Corporation of India Limited 94

Demurrage, Nature of Payment, Conduct 97

    33. Title: Larsen and Toubro Ltd *versus* Sunfield Resources Pvt Ltd 97

Demurrage, Exclusion Clauses, Interpretation 101

    34. Title: Steel Authority of India Limited *versus* Mercator Lines Limited 101

Arbitration, Incorporation Clause, Conduct 104

    35. Title: United Shippers Limited *versus* Tata Power Company Limited 104

Demurrage, Failure to Load, Foreseeability 106

    36. Title: William Henry Turner *versus* Kilburn and Co 106

Laytime, Weather Working Day, Meaning at Formation 108

    37. Title: Steel Authority of India *versus* Western Bulk Carriers KS 108

Laytime, Discharging Rate, Practicality 111

    38. Title: The Union of India *versus* The Great Eastern Shipping Co Ltd 111

Incorrect Shipping Mark, Bank Obligations, Unconditionality 114

    39. Title: Centax (India) Ltd versus Vinmar Impex Inc. 114

Laytime, Calculation, Evidence and Reasonability 116

    40. Title: PEC Limited *versus* ADM Asia Pacific Trading Pte Ltd 116

Performance Disputes in Shipping

Introduction

The title and table of contents are usually sufficient for this kind of literary work. Therefore, one could do without an introduction, but I feel it is important to provide context so that this book is as useful to the novice legal scholar, businessperson, foreign lawyer, or a beginner learner, as it is to a maritime law veteran.

These case notes are stories of performance disputes in shipping that came to be adjudicated in Indian courts. As such, they should not be read to understand the specific peculiarities of the law of procedure. They are insights into the substantive laws at play in these disputes. It is envisioned that the reader will consider the case notes relevant in determining whether further examination of the judgment is needed by them.

The book is divided into 3 parts by grouping the case notes into categories based on the main subject of the dispute; ship, cargo or documents. The headnotes of each of the case notes are created to indicate the event, cause of dispute, and determining factor. Thereafter, the essential identifiers have been mentioned: Title, Citation, and Court; where a judgment's citation is not available, the date of the judgment has been mentioned. All the case notes have been broken down into three sections; issue, facts, and analysis. All the three sections are a compression of the relevant judgment. The idea being that the reader is able to discern what happened in the dispute and what was the judgment of the Court.

Narration in the case notes follows the procedural story of the specific dispute so that it is clear whether the dispute was adjudicated in an arbitration first or in a Court directly. You will notice that where some facts are unimportant to the conclusion of the judgment, they have been omitted. For example: if a conclusion does not depend on an agent's actions then, the reference to the agent has been left out. Another example: where the volume of the cargo or the dates of the contracts do not matter, these have been omitted. However, to facilitate understanding of the social context, month and year of the event have been retained, where available.

Mainly Relating to Ship

<u>Redelivery Default, Expired Charterparty, Agreement by Conduct</u>

Title: Bharat Petroleum Corporation Ltd *versus* Great Eastern Shipping Co Ltd

Citation: (2008) 1 SCC 503

Court: Supreme Court of India

Issue:

This was an appeal from an order of a single judge of a High Court whereby they had set aside the award of an arbitral tribunal ruling that the tribunal had no jurisdiction to decide the dispute because there was no existing charterparty. The pertinent issue was whether the fact that the ship was in fact being used by the charterer after the expiration of the charterparty duration, coupled with their silence on the charter hire rate, be seen as acceptance of the previous charterparty terms.

Facts:

The ship *Jag Praja* was chartered for two years from 1996-1998 based on a charterparty drawn up in May 1997. In 1998, the charterparty was extended by mutual agreement for a period of two months. Post this, although the charterer continued to use the ship, no express agreement between the parties on the terms of a charterparty could be reached. It was the stance of the shipowner that the previous charterparty continued to exist, even though the duration stated in the charterparty had expired, because the charterer had continued to use the ship and had not redelivered it.

Analysis:

An offer is not accepted by mere silence on the part of the offeree, yet it does not mean that an acceptance is conveyed only by words. It can take the form of conduct in appropriate circumstances. Thus, where silence is coupled with a positive act, a *sub silentio* agreement develops. Therefore, the existence of a contract between the parties can be proved not only by their words but also by their conduct. Additionally, there was an obligation on the charterer to redeliver the ship to the shipowner on the expiration of the charterparty.

The Court found that during the course of communications between the parties, after the expiration of the previous charterparty and during the use of the ship by the charterer, the shipowner had informed the charterer that the usual practice, pending finalisation of a new charterparty, was that the existing terms and conditions continue to apply.

The conduct of the parties which included the charterer's continued use of the ship showed that, except for the charter rate, there was no other dispute between the parties. The charterer had agreed to the stand of the shipowner *sub silentio* and continued to bind themselves by the terms and conditions contained in the previous charterparty.

The arbitral tribunal had overlooked the clauses on 'redelivery' and 'final voyage'. A conjoint reading of these clauses obligated the charterer to redeliver the ship as per the procedure contemplated in the charterparty. Having failed to redeliver the ship, the charterer could not plead that the obligations arising from the charterparty had been discharged, merely because the period mentioned in the charterparty had come to an end. The factual scenario led to an inescapable conclusion that the expiry of the time period did not extinguish the effect of the charterparty.

Incompatible Port, Laytime, Responsibility

Title: Shipping Corporation of India Ltd *versus* Mare Shipping Inc

Citation: (2011) 8 SCC 39

Court: Supreme Court of India

Issue:

This was an appeal from an arbitration award in respect of liability to pay demurrage. The pertinent issue was who, the shipowner or the charterer, was responsible for verifying that the nominated port of discharge was compatible with the equipment of the ship. The answer to this issue would have answered whether the ship could be considered an arrived ship. The answers to these issues were pertinent to establish the validity of the Notice of Readiness (NoR), the calculation of laytime, and the subsequent demurrage claim.

Facts:

Through a charterparty of November 1999, the *MT Prestige* was chartered to carry crude oil for a trip from Ras Shukheir, Egypt, to 'one/two safe anchorage(s)/lighterage points/SBM(s)/one/two safe port(s)one/two safe berth(s) anywhere in India'. The vessel was described in the charterparty as being fitted with an 'AK Tongue Type Bow Chain Stopper of min SWL 2000 Mts'.

Subsequent to loading and commencement of the voyage to India, the charterer nominated a Single Berth Mooring (SBM) at Vadinar, Gujarat, India, as the discharge point. Upon reaching the anchorage of the Port of Vadinar, it was found that the mooring equipment on board the ship was not compatible with the SBM. Eventually the charterer, through an Addendum to the charterparty, agreed to divert the vessel to Mumbai, Maharashtra, India.

Post-discharge at Mumbai, the charterer contended that since the vessel could not be moored at Vadinar and because the destination was the SBM, not the anchorage, it was not an 'arrived ship' and could not have issued a valid NoR. Thus, they argued that laytime should not be calculated from Vadinar.

Analysis:

A ship is considered to have arrived at the right place when it has arrived at the place instructed by the charterer. If thereafter, it cannot load or discharge cargo due to incompatibility with the equipment at the place, the question of the validity of its arrival is dependent on the party responsible for the incompatibility. In a case where the Charterer is aware of the equipment of the vessel and they nominate the place of arrival, the responsibility for the incompatibility will lie with them.

A Clause obligated the Master to issue NoR after arrival at the 'customary anchorage' of the port. The Master did so and was thereafter informed of the incompatibility between the SBM and the vessel's equipment. The Court read that clause of the charterparty harmoniously with the Addendum holding that '(it was) abundantly clear that the charterer had accepted the responsibility for the failure of the vessel to discharge her cargo at Vadinar and had agreed to bear all the expenses for the delay in diversion of the vessel from Vadinar to Mumbai, including the time spent at Vadinar port and the expenses incurred towards pilotage, tugs and other port expenses'.

Crucially, the charterer had full knowledge of the equipment on board *MT Prestige* because it was so mentioned in the charterparty. Despite having such knowledge and subsequently, the charterer nominated the incompatible SBM as the point of discharge of the cargo.

In agreeing with the Arbitral Tribunal and subsequent Courts of appeal, the Court held that the responsibility for the failure of the ship to moor at the SBM lay squarely with the charterer as they nominated the SBM for the safe mooring of the vessel. Therefore, since the shipowner was not responsible for the incompatibility and subsequent diversion to Mumbai, laytime was held to have commenced at Vadinar after the expiry of the contractually agreed time from the tendering of the NoR. The charterer was liable to pay demurrage as claimed by the shipowner.

Dispossession of Ship, Omitted Lay Days, Reasonability

Title: Andrew Yule and Co *versus* Ardeshir Bomanji Dubash

Citation: AIR 1914 Bom 312 (2)

Court: High Court of Bombay

Issue:

This was an appeal from a decree of the trial Court dismissing the charterer's claim for injunction against the mortgagee of the ship. The relevant issue before the Court was whether the remaining charters were complete contracts even though the lay and cancelling dates were not specified in any of them.

Facts:

The charterer, involved in the coal trade between the cities of Bombay and Calcutta, and the shipowner entered into a charter agreement for the ship *Gymeric*. The agreement was for 12 consecutive voyages for which the parties executed 12 separate charterparty contracts.

The cancelling dates in the contracts in question were left blank and were to be filled-in after the completion of each voyage, by agreement. It was agreed that this was being done to allow the shipowner to commence the next voyage as soon as possible.

The *Gymeric* undertook 4 out of 12 voyages before the mortgagee of the ship sued the shipowner and gained possession of the ship. The charterer filed this suit to restrain the mortgagee from dealing with the vessel in any manner inconsistent with the remaining charterparty contracts. The mortgagee argued, amongst other things, that the remaining contracts were incomplete on account of omission to mention the lay and cancelling dates.

Analysis:

The charterer and the shipowner had specifically agreed to leave the lay and cancelling dates blank. The fact that this agreement was reached after the confirmation of the main charterparty terms was of no consequence. It was also of no value to the mortgagee to argue that the omission of those dates from the remaining contracts invalidated them on account of incompleteness because it is generally understood that those dates are for the protection of the charterer.

The Court also held that this omission did not present a major problem because it would be easy to find that the lay days commence within a reasonable date of the arrival of the ship in the port of loading. Consequentially, the cancelling date would be within a reasonable time thereafter. The parties had mentioned what dates would be reasonable in the first charterparty contract. They had also adhered to the same measure of reasonability in the three subsequent contracts. Therefore, it was difficult to hold that the omission had a meaningful consequence on the contracts and certainly not the one that the mortgagee claimed. The decree of the trial Court was set aside and the injunction claimed by the charterer was granted.

Engine Breakdown, Laytime Calculation, Scope of Clause

Title: Steel Authority of India Ltd *versus* Pacific Gulf Shipping Co Ltd

Citation: 2013 SCC Online Bom 1238

Court: High Court of Bombay

Issue:

This was an appeal from a decision of a single judge who had dismissed a petition challenging an arbitral award granting demurrage payment to the shipowner. The pertinent issue was whether the period which followed an engine breakdown could be excluded from the calculation of laytime when the responsibility to berth was the charterer's.

Facts:

MV Navios Sagitarrius was chartered in November 2010 to carry a consignment of coking coal in bulk from DBCT, QLD, Australia, to Vizag, Paradip, and Haldia, India. This dispute was in relation to the discharge at Vizag. The charterer was obligated to obtain a berth at the port. On entering port limits, laytime started counting 24 hours after the Notice of Readiness was served. The ship was unable to berth because of engine failure. After it was repaired, it took some time to re-berth. In the meantime, the charterer allowed a different ship to berth. The charterer contended that the entire period from engine failure till re-berthing, including the period spent idle waiting for the other ship to leave berth, was to be excluded from laytime calculation. The arbitral tribunal only excluded the period relating to engine failure. The single judge affirmed the arbitral tribunal's decision on the ground that it constituted a fair interpretation of the terms of the charterparty by experts.

Analysis:

The charterer's main argument was that the word 'equipment' in the charterparty clause on the exclusion of laytime meant only 'discharge equipment'. The charterer contended that 'engine' was not to be read into the term 'equipment of the vessel'. However, at the time of execution of the charterparty, the parties had consciously chosen to delete the words 'gears/cranes/winches and' from this clause. Therefore, the charterer's interpretation was rightfully denied by the arbitral tribunal. The Court, as well as the arbitral tribunal, was not willing to expand the scope of this clause to cover the period during which the ship waited for the other ship to leave berth. The charterer was in a difficult situation because, having allowed another ship to berth, they were also not left with a remedy in damages.

Dysfunctional Equipment, Validity of NoR, Specified Consequences

Title: Steel Authority of India (SAIL) *versus* Dampskibaselsbaket Norden

Citation: 2014 (211) DLT 324

Court: High Court of Delhi

Issue:

This was an appeal by the charterer challenging an arbitration award in favour of the shipowner. The issue before the Court was whether the charterer could claim invalidity of the Notice of Readiness (NoR) on the basis of the fact that the ships arrived at their discharge ports with dysfunctional cranes. The arbitral tribunal had accepted the shipowner's alternate suggestion for pro-rata deduction from laytime calculation.

Facts:

In March 2008, a Contract of Affreightment (COA) was executed between the shipowner and the charterer for transporting coking coal from Virginia, United States of America, to Vishakhapatnam, Paradip, and Haldia, India, through three shipments. The dispute was in respect of the carriage of two shipments by the ships *MV Nord Fighter* and *MV Navios Kypros*. Both ships were to discharge part of their cargoes at Vishakhapatnam and, subsequently, at Haldia. *MV Nord Fighter* had reached the first port of discharge with a dysfunctional grab. *MV Navios Kypros* had suffered a crane breakdown during discharge at the first port. The Charterer relied on a clause of the charterparty, a time counting provision, to state that both the NoRs were invalid because the vessels were not 'ready in all respects to discharge the cargo.' Consequently, they dishonoured the shipowner's laytime calculations and, subsequent, demurrage claims. The shipowner claimed, relying on other clauses of the charterparty, that the cranes' issue could only give rise to pro-rata deduction of time from the laytime calculations and did not affect the validity of the NoRs or running of laytime.

Analysis:

Delivering the NoR is a symbolic event which indicates the transfer of responsibility of operations from the shipowner to the charterer. Thus, an invalidated NoR would reflect the continuity of the shipowner's period of responsibility and this would have obvious financial consequences.

The COA did not state that all cranes must be available for discharge, nor did it state that if any crane is not operational, the NoR is not valid. The contractual term 'ready in all respects to discharge the cargo' signified a requirement of readiness. However, these words did not indicate that the 'vessel(s) should be ready to discharge cargo at the discharge rate provided in the charterparty.' This was a strict interpretation of the term. The alternate interpretation, given by the arbitral tribunal, that 'as long as the vessel can discharge' was reasonable and probable.

This was also not a case where all the cranes were not working. If that was the case, a different consequence would have followed. But in this case, since the contract provided for a remedy, in case the rate of discharge was not met, it was telling that the breakdown of one or two cranes would not attract the Charterer's interpretation.

The charterparty clauses on laytime helped deny the charterer's interpretation because they showed that where laytime was to be excluded, the charterparty specifically provided for the same. There was no clause for laytime to be excluded for a breakdown of cranes. If the parties had intended to stop laytime because of the breakdown of a crane, they would have expressly provided for the same. This view was strengthened by the fact that they made a provision for pro-rata deduction which showed that such a contingency was within their contemplation. Since whatever is omitted is considered to be excluded, it was a plausible and reasonable view that the parties did not intend to stop laytime because of a dysfunctional crane.

The Court studied older cases to see whether all the cranes had to be functioning, for the vessel to be in such a state of readiness that without it an NoR could not be considered valid. In those cases, there were express conditions on the issuance of an NoR, with other provisions which effectively 'contracted out' the conditions by stipulating some consequences for their breach without invalidating the NOR. In the present case, there was no express condition that four working cranes of stipulated capacity were to be ensured by the shipowner before tendering the NoR. Even if it was assumed that there was such a condition, the fact that there were clauses attaching specific consequences to the breach demonstrated the intention of the parties to contract out of it and, similarly, leave the NoR unaffected.

The broad interpretation by the Charterer of the words, 'period of such insufficiency' in the clause, relating to gear/crane breakdown was commercially unreasonable and it was also inconsistent with the scheme of the COA. It had to be read in harmony with the clauses relating to discharge rate to mean that the consequence of the breakdown of a crane would be a proportional reduction in laytime during the breakdown period. This was a commercially reasonable interpretation. On the other hand, the charterers' interpretation was unreasonable because it effectively led to the conclusion that laytime should not count even though the other three cranes were functioning and discharging cargo. The tribunal's award was right on this issue.

Additionally, the charterer argued that demurrage should also be reduced on a pro-rata basis even though there was no clause to this effect in the COA. The charterer wanted to make use of the clause in respect of laytime reduction due to machinery breakdown and asked for its application to the pre-berthing period. The Court identified that a voyage charter has four stages: (1) the loading voyage, (2) the loading operation, (3) the carrying voyage, and (4) the discharging operation. Laytime applied to the operation stages and did not start till the time the voyage stages had ended. Once it started, there were only specific reasons for which it could be stopped. In the present case, a whether-in-berth-or-not (WIBON) clause made the laytime start once the NoR was tendered after the ships were in port and even if they were not at berth. This meant that laytime started to count during the pre-berthing period. The clause in respect of laytime reduction due to machinery breakdown transferred the risk of delay from the charterer back to the shipowner. There were no words in this clause that confined its operation to the post-berthing period nor evidenced an intent to restrict its effect to the period that the ships were alongside a berth. This being the position, the shipowner could not have gained a greater advantage than if the ships were at berth. The charterer was correctly entitled to pro-rata reduction in respect of its demurrage payment.

Withdrawal of Ship, Hire Payment Deductions, Possessory Rights

Title: Indian Oil Corporation Ltd *versus* Thakur Shipping Co Ltd

Citation: ILR 1974 Delhi 650

Court: High Court of Delhi

Issue:

This was an appeal from an order that restrained the shipowner from hiring out their vessel to anyone else. The pertinent issue was whether the Charterer possessed a right which denied the shipowner from exercising their contractual right to withdraw? The other important issue was whether the Charterer had a strong *prima facie* case to ask for such a restraint on the shipowner's right?

Facts:

In February 1973, a charterparty was executed to hire the ship, *Varuna Kanchan,* for a period of 24 months to carry oil from Iraq to India. It stated that the hire was strictly payable in advance at the commencement of the calendar month. A few months after the commencement of the charter, the Charterer made an advance hire payment after deducting some amounts from it. The shipowner responded with a notice disputing the Charterer's right to deduct those amounts, demanding full payment of hire, and reserving its right to withdraw the ship. Since the Charterer refused to make payment, the ship was withdrawn from their services.

The charterer then initiated arbitration proceedings, but, by this time, the shipowner had already hired the ship out to a new charterer. Both parties approached the Court to determine whether the shipowner had validly exercised their right to withdraw the ship from the services of the charterer.

Analysis:

A charter, not by demise, is where the charterer does not get any proprietary or possessory rights in the ship i.e. the charterer is only receiving services for payment. A time charterer has no proprietary or possessory rights in the ship by virtue of the charterparty. The Court highlighted that possessory rights were gained by virtue of a demise charterparty but not by a time charterparty. The charterparty in this case was not a demise charterparty because the employees of the shipowner were in-charge of the ship. The charterer only had a contractual right to the services of the ship but no interest in it.

On a *prima facie* view, the Court found that the deductions made by the charterer were not warranted by the express terms of the charterparty. The evidence also showed that the charterer's factual assertions for those deductions were not sound. There were glaring fundamental errors made in making the deductions.

The charterer's argument that the shipowner should have objected to the deductions and asked for settlement of disputes in the next payment failed, because this was not the procedure laid down in the clause relating to payment of hire. This clause also provided for the 'clear' right of the shipowner to withdraw the vessel from service if default of hire payment had occurred. All that was required by this clause was default on payment by the charterer and service of notice to the charterer.

The charterer's argument, that the shipowner's action of not withdrawing the ship till the unloading was ongoing, after service of notice, and of appropriating partial payment, was a waiver of their right to withdraw, also failed. The Court noted that the ship was withdrawn as soon as loading was completed, and the shipowner had appropriated partial payment after informing the charterer of their intention to withdraw. These were unequivocal acts which safeguarded the shipowner's right to withdraw. As per the Court, the charterer had no *prima facie* case to restrain the shipowner.

The charterer also argued for injunction on the basis that the charterparty contained a negative covenant that implied that the ship could not be hired to anyone else till the current charter survived. However, the charterer had relied on judicial precedents in which the charterer had possession of the ship, unlike the present case. The charterer, having failed to perform their part of the obligation to pay, could not ask for an injunction against the shipowner on the reasoning that they were committing a breach of a negative covenant. The charterer's remedy for damages remained available to them.

Cancellation of Carriage, Concluded Contract, Express Terms and Intention

Title: Trimex International FZE Ltd Dubai *versus* Vedanta Aluminium Ltd India

Citation: (2010) 3 SCC 1

Court: Supreme Court of India

Issue:

This was a petition by a charterer for the appointment of an arbitrator, to adjudicate a dispute with the buyer of cargo who refused to accept that there was a binding contract between the parties. The issue before the Court was whether the correspondence between the parties showcased an intention to be bound by the discussed terms and therefore, by the arbitration clause within this correspondence?

Facts:

In 2007, the charterer hired ships to supply Bauxite from Australia to Vizag/Kakinada, India, to the buyer. It was envisioned that there would be 5 shipments. After the first shipment, the buyer communicated to the charterer that they must defer other shipments. The charterer terminated the charterparty with the shipowner. It also had to compensate the shipowner for losses and damages due to the termination. The charterer claimed the amount of that compensation from the buyer and initiated arbitration.

The buyer argued that there was no concluded contract between the parties for the latter 4 shipments. They claimed that the first shipment had been sent on the basis of a commercial offer that was followed up with a purchase order. The purchase order, they claimed, was 'executed by and between the parties'. They claimed that the only agreed element was that there would be 5 shipments. Therefore, they claimed, that the emails exchanged between the parties did not amount to a concluded contract and they were not bound to accede to the charterer's demand for the appointment of an arbitrator.

Analysis:

Once a contract is concluded orally or in writing, the mere fact that a formal contract was to be prepared and initialled by the parties would not affect the validity of the acceptance of the contract or affect the performance thereof. Even if the formal contract was never initialled.

The email correspondence showed that the charterer's commercial offer contained a clause that stated 'this contract is governed by Indian law and arbitration in Mumbai Courts'. The buyer never made any comments on this clause. Additionally, it was clear from the correspondence that a valid acceptance had been made by the buyer since all essential ingredients of the contract had been informed to them. This was patent from a response from the buyer that stated 'we confirm the deal for five shipments'. These words showed that the buyer understood all the details and then confirmed the terms of the contract. The buyer's argument that the clauses were unclear and ambiguous was unacceptable because the buyer's acceptance was unconditional and unqualified. They were not entitled to escape the obligations that flowed from their acceptance.

It was also material that the commercial offer did not carry a clause that made conclusion of the contract dependent upon a purchase order. A lack of it could, thus, not be taken as a defence to the formation of the contract. There was nothing to show that the parties did not intend to be bound by the discussed terms.

The argument by the buyer that the lack of a signed contract made the arbitration clause unenforceable was rejected because there was judicial precedent to show that such a requirement did not exist in law.

Expiry of Term of Performance, Laycan, Reasonability

Title: Steel Authority of India Ltd *versus* Jaldhi Overseas Pte Ltd

Citation: 2021 SCC Online Del 3002

Court: High Court of Delhi

Issue:

This was a petition challenging an arbitral award in favour of the carrier. The pertinent issue was whether the words, 'likely commencement in July 2017' in a contract of affreightment (CoA) were to be understood as meaning immediately, within the month, or anytime afterwards? The answer to this issue had implications for the term of performance of the contract, and other obligations relating to holiday and extension.

Facts:

The parties entered into a CoA in June 2017, to transport a cargo of limestone from Mina Saqr Port, Ras Al Khaimah, United Arab Emirates, to the ports of Vishakhapatnam/ Gangavarnam/ Paradip/ Haldia, India. It was agreed that this would be done through several shipments. The consignee declared its first laycan in September 2017, three months after the CoA. In June 2018, one year after the CoA, the consignee emailed the carrier demanding a shipment holiday and asking for an extension of the delivery period. In response, the carrier informed the consignee that it could not do so because it was the last month of the term of the CoA. The consignee argued that the term of the CoA began when the first laycan was declared in September 2017. They then claimed entitlement to a term which survived for 12 months i.e. till September 2018. The parties referred their dispute to an arbitral tribunal which refused to accept the consignee's arguments.

Analysis:

A commercial contract has to be construed through the application of the reasonably minded commercial person test.

It was the consignee's case that the words, 'likely commencement in July 2017', did not restrict their right to declare the first laycan. They claimed that it was not necessary to make the first shipment in the month of July 2017. This was contrary to their emails which evidenced an understanding that they would request for nomination of vessels for shipment immediately after the execution of the CoA. The arbitral tribunal was justified in interpreting that those words showcased an agreement to make the first shipment in the month of July 2017. The tribunal's view was reasonable and this meant that the term of the CoA would run up till July 2018. The clause in which these words existed could not be interpreted to mean that the period of twelve months could be extended indefinitely.

The consignee had also failed to follow the contractual procedure stipulated for demanding the shipment holiday and an extension of the delivery period. Therefore, they lost the right to claim the benefits of these provisions. Their demand came at the end of June 2018, the last month of the term of the CoA, whereas the contractual procedure was that the consignee should inform the carrier of the shipment holiday at least one month prior to expiry. They should have exercised this option by the end of May 2018. Their demand was, thus, invalid.

The consignee had also faulted in demanding an extension of the delivery period by demanding it in a sequential order from the shipment holiday. Therefore, the demand for extension could not be read on a standalone basis. Since the demand for shipment holiday was invalid, the logical conclusion was that the demand for extension was also invalid. Even otherwise, the contractual procedure for demanding an extension required the consignee to inform the carrier at least one month prior to the expiry of agreed/auto-extended delivery schedule. This was, clearly, not done. It was pertinent that the consignee had not demanded any shipments to be made in the month of July 2018. Their demand for a shipment to be made in August 2018, fell out of the agreed period of delivery.

Frustrated Charterparty, Advance Freight, Domestic Law

Title: Gandha Korliah *versus* Janoo Hassan

Citation: ILR (1926) 49 Mad 200

Court: High Court of Madras

Issue:

This was an appeal, arising from a judgment in favour of the charterer, to receive back the advance freight paid on a frustrated charterparty. The pertinent question was whether the nature of the payment was such that only maritime law applied to it? The answer to this question would have helped determine whether the claim of the charterer attracted Indian law of general contract.

Facts:

In 1919, two ships were chartered to carry bags of rice from Sittwe (formerly Akyab), Myanmar, to ports in South India (formerly Madras Presidency). The charterer paid partial freight as advance according to the terms of the charterparty. Although the ships were ready to load at Akyab, the necessary cargoes could not be provided. This was due to a government order that prohibited the export of rice without a license. Neither of the parties had guaranteed obtaining the license. It was the case of the charterer, that the advance freight paid by them be returned on account of frustration of contract. The shipowner argued that they were a common carrier and only maritime law provisions from England applied to them, under which advance freight was irrecoverable.

Analysis:

The shipowner argued that contracts with common carriers were of a special kind that were out of the scope of governance of the Indian Contract Act, 1872. However, the Court opined that since the ships in the present case were on charter, they could not be categorised as common carriers. A common carrier is a general ship taking the goods of several shippers under separate bills of lading on the same voyage.

The underlying argument of the shipowner was that peculiar features of the present contract were only governable under English common law. However, this argument failed to take into consideration that the shipowner and charterer were Indian. Their relation was not one that had to be seen only in the confines of a maritime contract. Additionally, English judicial precedent made it clear that the inability to recover advance freight on the frustration of the venture was a principle derived from English common law, not from maritime contracts. Thus, there was no reason to treat the dispute as being excluded from the application of the law of the country in which it was situated i.e. India. Applying the Indian Contract Act, 1872, it was clear that advance freight had to be returned because of frustration of the contract.

Delivery Default, Role of Disponent Owner, Remedy

Title: Epoch Enterrepots *versus* MV Won Fu

Citation: (2003) 1 SCC 305

Court: Supreme Court of India

Issue:

This was an appeal from an order of a High Court division bench dismissing the charterer's suit and releasing the vessel. The issue was whether the breach of the terms of a fixture note, agreed with the disponent owner, gave rise to a claim in rem against the ship. The narrower issue was whether the fixture note alone evidenced that the disponent owner is a demise charterer.

Facts:

In October 1995, the charterer signed a fixture note with the disponent owner for transportation of a cargo of Feldspar from Tuticorin, India, to Taiwan, on the vessel *MV Won Fu*. The vessel discharged an earlier cargo at Madras Port, India, and was to arrive at Tuticorin. The ship did not arrive at Tuticorin. The charterer filed a suit against the ship, for failure to act in terms of the fixture note, and asked for losses that occurred by reason of a deliberate act of default to ship the cargo on the vessel.

This suit was dismissed by the original Court on the basis that it was wrongly filed against the ship and not the disponent owner. The

Court ruled that the charterer could not show that a contract with the ship's owner existed. Therefore, there was no justification for arrest, or for a suit under the admiralty jurisdiction of the Court. A subsequent appeal was dismissed by the High Court.

Analysis:

A fixture note by itself is not sufficient evidence that the party signing it is a demise charterer i.e. a party possessing and controlling the ship.

On the facts of the case, as evidenced, the disponent owner was not a demise charterer. The fixture note was issued on the possibility of a future charter of the vessel. Conclusively, there was no right to proceed with their case under the in-rem jurisdiction of admiralty Courts in India. This left the charterer in a poor position because they could not arrest the ship on the basis of the fixture note. The correct remedy was to approach the proper forum against the disponent owner.

The charterer's argument, that by virtue of no show by the ship a maritime lien came into existence, was also not accepted by the Court. There was substantial past judicial and academic writing to support this conclusion.

Draft Charterparty, Condition to Formation, Intention

Title: Rickmers Verwaltung GmbH *versus* Indian Oil Corporation Ltd

Citation: (1999) 1 SCC 1

Court: Supreme Court of India

Issue:

This was an appeal from a High Court order, restraining the shipowner from proceeding with arbitration on a finding that there was no binding charterparty between the parties. The issue before the Court was whether a drawn up charterparty was binding. The narrower issue was about the effect of lack of agreement on letter of credit and performance guarantee.

Facts:

Sometime in 1993, the alleged charterer invited offers for transportation of pipes from Tampico, Mexico, to India. The shipowner responded with an offer. However, correspondence ensued about the format of the letter of credit (LoC) and language of the performance guarantee (PG). A charterparty was drawn-up but it was not signed. The dates for loading were informed to the shipowner. These dates were missed as the correspondence continued without agreement. Finally, the alleged charterer informed the shipowner that they were making alternative arrangements due to the shipowner's failure to carry out their obligations. The shipowner, relying on a clause of the drawn-up charterparty, invoked arbitration for losses.

The shipowner argued, that the drawn-up charterparty along with the correspondence should be viewed as a binding contract. The alleged charterer countered by stating that there was no agreement on fundamental requirements, the LoC and PG. Thus, there was no concluded charterparty and no arbitration agreement ever came into existence.

Analysis:

The negotiation of the terms of a charterparty need to conclude for them to be binding i.e. enforceable.

The draft charterparty stated that freight, the consideration in a contract of transportation, was payable through a standby irrevocable LoC. The Court needed to see whether this clause stood out as a condition precedent to the formation of contract. For this, it studied the correspondence, mainly fax messages, between the alleged charterer and the shipowner. This correspondence, unmistakably, evidenced that the two parties did not agree on proceeding further till there was agreement on the LoC and PG.

The correspondence continued beyond the loading date and evidenced the shipowner's categorical disagreement to the LoC. The shipowner, through its agent, had consistently maintained the stance that their offer was subject to acceptance of the LoC. This showcased that the shipowner interpreted the LoC to be a condition precedent to the formation of contract.

Having come to this conclusion, the Court also found that the language of the correspondence was so clear that no inverse interpretation could be made in favour of the shipowner's argument. The correspondence did not evidence an intent to be mutually bound to the terms of the charterparty, before agreement on the LoC. This had to emerge unequivocally and clearly from the correspondence. At best, the parties were negotiating. When parties are at the stage of negotiation, they do not bind each other to the contract. The negotiations in this case never completed by virtue of no agreement being reached. Therefore, the Court denied the shipowner's case.

Redelivery Default, Off Hire Clause, Ordinary Meaning

Title: Wizdoms Naik International Limited *versus* DSV Gerimal (IMO No 7932240)

Citation: 2020 SCC OnLine Bom 7647

Court: High Court of Bombay

Issue:

This was an application filed by the charterer for vacating arrest of a ship. The issue before the Court was whether the shipowner's claim for hire payments was made as per the charterparty. The pertinent issue was whether the vessel remained on hire after the charterer had failed to redeliver it.

Facts:

Sometime in 2016, *Ocean 303*, an all-weather barge was hired by the charterer off the coast of Mumbai for a period of 165 days. After this period, it was to be re-delivered to a port in the United Arab Emirates (UAE) by the charterer. The charterer did not do so and used the barge for many months after the expiration of the charter period. In the meantime, the charterer and the shipowner entered into negotiations for a subsequent charterparty, but these negotiations did not materialise. Correspondingly, the shipowner demanded that the charterer pay on-hire charges, that were calculated per day, as per the expired charterparty. The clause relating to off-hire read as follows:

> 41.11 Off-hire is done once vessel is re-delivered to delivery port as per box 8 and free of charterers men and material.

The charterer did not do so. Consequentially to realise its claim, the shipowner arrested one of the ships of the charterer, *DSV Gerimal*. The charterer argued that the shipowner was not entitled to claim on-hire charges after the expiration of the charter period.

Analysis:

Express clauses of the charterparty have to be given their ordinary and unambiguous meaning. If conditions of a particular clause are not met, then the question of the clause applying would not arise.

The charterer argued, that the shipowner was not entitled to on-hire payment for the subsequent days that the barge remained with the charterer. Instead, they argued, the shipowner would have been entitled to the amount of charter hire that they would have earned for a voyage from Mumbai to UAE. Essentially, they argued that the vessel was redelivered but not to the right port. They further argued that since another clause of the charterparty made the redelivery voyage from Mumbai to UAE free, the shipowner was not even entitled to this amount. For these arguments, the charterer relied on past judicial precedent where redelivery had to be made at a safe port and the question of damages arose in respect of the default to make such a redelivery.

The charterer's reliance on the past judicial precedent was entirely misplaced because in the present case redelivery was not done at all. Clause 41.11 made it clear that until the barge was redelivered to the specified port, and the charterer's men and material had been off-loaded, the vessel would be treated as on-hire. This was plainly and unambiguously what the clause meant. The fact that the parties had contracted in this fashion made them liable to be bound by the clauses. The existence of this clause dissipated any reason to go into the question of damages, a remedy which would have come to the shipowner's rescue in case there was no clause.

It also did not help the charterer to argue that the shipowner had not raised any invoices for the hire payment relating to this period. The existence of the charterparty, contemporaneous communication putting the charterer at notice of the redelivery period, and contemporaneous communication during the negotiations of the subsequent charterparty through which the shipowner reserved its right, were sufficient for establishing the claim.

Finally, the charterer's request to allow for movement of the ship under arrest, in Indian territorial waters, was also rejected. This was because they had failed to lay a foundation for this request. Merely pleading that the ship was required for work in another commercial activity was not sufficient. The charterer should have brought on record the relevant contract(s) and adequate material. It was also telling that the charterer did not produce any evidence of a class survey or dry dock, making it doubtful that the ship could even ply for such purposes. Nor had the charterer produced any evidence of the condition of the ship's hull and machinery and insurance. In light of these circumstances, allowing the ship to move meant putting it in peril. The arrest was maintained.

Performance Disputes in Shipping

Delay, Risk Allocation, Contract Terms

Title: Bridge Marine Ltd *versus* Indian Oil Corporation Limited

Date: 16th June 2021

Court: High Court of Delhi

Issue:

This was a challenge by the shipowner to an arbitral award denying them compensation for delay. The issue was, when did the shipowner's obligation end and when did the charterer's obligations begin? The pertinent issue was whether the non-issuance of a Notice of Readiness (NoR) disallowed the ship from being considered as having arrived at the port of loading?

Facts:

In December 2013, the *MT Cosmic Jewel* was chartered to transport a cargo of crude oil from Yoho and Bonga, Nigeria, to Vadinar, India. Loading at Yoho happened first and then the vessel proceeded to Bonga. When the vessel arrived at a pilot station before the port of Bonga, it was denied inward clearance because no berth was available, and the cargo was not ready for loading. The vessel waited at the pilot station for 15.5 days. All this while, the Master did not issue an NoR. In due course and after the shipment of the cargo had been completed, the shipowner raised a claim for compensation for the delay that took place at the pilot station. They argued that as per clause 9 of the charterparty, it was the charterer's obligation to ensure that the berth was available, and the inward clearance was provided. Without this obligation being performed first, a valid NoR could not be issued. The charterer argued that their obligation to provide a berth only activated after the NoR had been issued as per clause 6.

Clause 6. Notice of Readiness.

Upon arrival at customary anchorage at each port of loading or discharge, the Master or his agent shall give Charterer or his agent, notice by letter, telegraph, wireless or telephone that the Vessel is ready to load or discharge cargo, berth or no berth, and laytime, as hereinafter provided, shall commence upon the expiration of six (6) hours after receipt of such notice, or upon the Vessel's arrival in berth (i.e., finished mooring when at sealoading or discharging terminal and all fast when loading or discharging alongside a wharf), whichever first occurs. However, where delay is caused to Vessel getting into berth after giving Notice of Readiness for any reason over which Charterer has no control, such delay shall not count as used laytime.

Clause 9. Safe Berthing-Shifting.

The Vessel shall load and discharge at any safe place or wharf, or alongside vessels or lighters reachable on her arrival, which shall be designated and procured by the Charterer, provided the Vessel can proceed thereto, lie at, and depart therefrom always safely afloat, any lighterage being at the expense, risk and peril of the Charterer.

Analysis:

Contractual terms evidence the allocation of risk, and the method of shifting risk between parties at the time of formation of the contract. These terms cannot be invalidated with arguments on a later date.

The legal position in respect of activation of obligations in port charters is more difficult than in more specific charters like berth charters. This difficulty arises due to the vastness of ports and divergent practices, such as pilotage, at each individual port. Sometimes, like in the present case, confusion can brew whether the vessel has arrived at the correct place. Once the ship is considered an arrived ship according to the terms of the charterparty, it is obligated to issue a NoR to the charterer.

This was a case of a port charter. The shipowner, through the Master, had failed to issue an NoR when the vessel arrived at the pilot station before Bonga. During the arbitration, the shipowner admitted that this pilot station was the usual waiting place for vessels before proceeding into the limits of the port of Bonga. There was clear judicial precedent for the proposition that a vessel in a usual waiting area will be considered an arrived ship. It did not matter if this waiting area was outside the port or inside it. The shipowner's strict interpretation of the words 'customary anchorage' in clause 6 was incorrect. The arbitral tribunal was correct in holding that the pilot station which acted as the usual waiting place was to be considered customary anchorage.

The Master had, by non-issuance of the NoR, committed a mistake for which the charterer could not be made liable. The clauses of the charterparty were to be read harmoniously and therefore, the charterer's obligation to provide a berth only arose after the NoR had been issued post arrival. The shipowner's mistake, through the Master, of not considering the vessel as arrived left it remedy-less for the 15.5 days it waited at the pilot station. The tribunal correctly noted that there was no other pre-condition expressed in the charterparty in relation to issuance of the NoR. The shipowner should have issued an NoR when the vessel arrived at the pilot station.

Their argument that the words 'reachable on arrival' in clause 9 meant that the arrival of the ship depended on the availability of the berth, could not be sustained. This was counteracted by clause 6 which provided for issuance of NoR at customary anchorage 'berth or no berth'.

Additionally, there was judicial precedent to the effect that when a ship reaches a usual waiting place, a presumption arises of charterer's effective disposition over the ship. The lack of issuance of a NoR did not allow for this presumption to be utilised by the shipowner.

Refusal to Load, Disponent Owner, Admiralty Jurisdiction

Title: MV Leonis *versus* Libra Shipping Services LLC

Citation: 2009 SCC OnLine Guj 8718

Court: High Court of Gujarat

Issue:

This was an application challenging a suit filed against the ship for claims against the disponent owner. The issue before the Court was whether the suit could be sustained in light of the fact that the disponent owner was not the head-owner of the ship?

Facts:

In October 2006, the *MV Leonis* was chartered on a voyage charter from the disponent owner to take cargo from Kandla, India, to Japan. At the time of loading, the charterer was informed that Japan was an excluded trading area. Dismayed by this turn of events, the charterer filed a suit against the vessel and the disponent owner claiming breach of charterparty. In the suit, the charterer prayed for arrest of bunkers in the vessel, claiming that the bunkers were owned by the disponent owner. In addition, they also prayed for arrest of the vessel. The vessel was arrested and subsequently released on payment of security. In the meantime, the dispute between the charterer and disponent owner was also referred to arbitration in London as per terms of their charterparty. In this application, the head-owner argued that the suit was not maintainable against the ship on the basis of a claim against the disponent owner.

Analysis:

The power of arrest of a ship under admiralty jurisdiction of a Court is exercisable against certain statutorily identified actors, it cannot be extended to cover others.

The Court identified that admiralty jurisdiction, of which an important power is to arrest a ship, against the ship was invoked by the charterer on the basis of a claim against the disponent owner. It was hard to see how the Court's admiralty jurisdiction and specifically the power of arrest could be invoked against the ship. More fundamentally, the charterer was not able to prove that they had any privity of contract with the head-owner. The charterer only had a contract with the disponent owner. This gave them a right against the disponent owner but not against the ship. The suit was rejected, and the security paid by the head-owner was ordered to be returned.

Failure to Mobilise, Bank Guarantee, Separability

Title: Rolv Berg Drive A/S *versus* Oil and Natural Gas Corporation Ltd

Citation: 2007 SCC Online Bom 1577

Court: High Court of Bombay

Issue:

This was an appeal against an order of a single judge declining the shipowner's request to prevent the charterer from encashing a bank backed performance guarantee. The issue before the Court was whether a guideline passed by the shipowner's government was sufficient to invoke the force majeure provision of the charterparty?

Facts:

In February 2007, the *MV Aldoma*, was hired by the charterer to perform several functions in their offshore operations. The *MV Aldoma* was an anchor handling tug. The charter document stated the scope of work as towing, carrying men and material, standby and rescue, exigency assistance, routine surveillance, mooring assistance, and other field work. It also stated that the above functions 'shall always be performed within the vessel's natural capabilities and within safe parameters'. The charter document also required the shipowner to furnish a bank backed performance guarantee. This was duly furnished. Consequently, and a day prior to the mobilisation date, the shipowner informed the charterer of their inability to provide the vessel. In response, the charterer moved to encash the performance guarantee.

Analysis:

The shipowner claimed that as per a guideline issued by the Government of Norway, the country of registration of the vessel, the vessel was unsuitable to be employed in water depths that were required by the charterer. For this, they relied on the force majeure clause in the charter document which made provision for 'Acts and Regulations of the respective Governments'. They argued that since force majeure events made the charter contract impossible, the performance guarantee also lost its ability to be encashed.

In response, the charterer argued that the shipowner had taken the vessel to Nigeria and were merely using the force majeure clause as a shield. They argued that the vessel was not required only for those water depths but had other uses too. The usage of the vessel for any particular work was first sanctioned by an expert agency; this was stated in the contract document. Finally, they argued that none of this affected their right to encash the bank backed performance guarantee.

The Court found force in the charterer's arguments. The Court found that the shipowner was not able to produce any evidence that would clarify the nature of the guidelines issued by the Norwegian Government. Crucially, it remained unproven whether those guidelines were directory or mandatory. Given the wide scope of work for which the vessel was needed, the shipowner was not able to prove if the guidelines completely disabled its employment.

It was also telling that the shipowner, themselves, had informed the charterer of the vessel being taken to Nigeria. Thereafter, the shipowner made an offer of a substitute vessel. The Court found that this sequence of events was not in favour of the shipowner. Even at the Court's asking, the shipowner was not able to provide a substitute vessel of the same specifications.

The single judge was correct in holding, that the performance guarantee could be encashed at the charterer's option. It was an independent contract between the bank and the charterer. It was not dependant on the underlying contract, the charter document. It was possible to prevent the encashment of the guarantee on proof of fraud or irretrievable injustice. However, the shipowner was not able to prove either. Pertinently, the shipowner's position was protected by the arbitration clause in the charter document. It enabled them to seek refund of the encashed amount on successfully establishing their claim in arbitration. The order of the single judge was upheld in favour of the charterer.

Mainly Relating to Cargo

Slack Bags, Unknown Weight, Burden of Proof

Title: Thakur Shipping Co Ltd Bombay *versus* Food Corporation of India

Citation: AIR 1983 MADRAS 105

Court: High Court of Madras

Issue:

This was an appeal from a decision of a subordinate judge that held the carrier responsible for the amount of short-landed goods when measured by weight. The bills of lading, issued pursuant to a charterparty, mentioned the number of bags and an express stipulation that their weight was unknown. The pertinent question before the Court was about the effect of the 'weight unknown' clause on the liability of the carrier.

Facts:

The ship, *SS Varunadevi*, was chartered to carry 96,000 bags of Thai Rice from Bangkok, Thailand, to Tuticorin, India. The mate's receipts and the bills of lading evidenced that the bags were loaded onto the ship. During discharge, it was noticed that some of the bags were slack i.e. that they had lost weight. The charterer-consignee alleged that the carrier was responsible for the loss.

Analysis:

The enquiry into the liability of the carrier has traditionally depended upon a finding of whether it is a common carrier or not, because a common carrier has a higher standard of care than a special carrier. The identity of the carrier can be identified by seeing whether its ship is employed as a general ship by several shippers or is under a charter. In the present case, there was a special contract, the charterparty, and therefore, the carrier was not a common carrier. The question of liability of the carrier had to be determined on the basis of the charterparty.

On reviewing previous authorities, the Court found that the law was clear that if the bill of lading, functioning as a receipt of goods, mentioned the number of bags, tins, or containers, that are shipped then that would constitute sufficient evidence against the carrier. However, where more complicated information such as 'weight, contents, and value' are concerned, if the bill of lading had a qualifying remark that these were unknown, then the carrier was not bound by statements in their regard. Resultantly, the charterer-consignee had to prove that the consignments loaded on board the ship were of the same weight, the contents were of the same nature, and the value was of the same figure, as those noted in the bills of lading. The logic was that the verification of the number of bags was easy and did not involve any complicated process. Whereas the verification of weight or nature or the value of goods would have required specialised tests and also proven to be a time-consuming exercise that would not be feasible in shipping operations.

In the present case, the carrier undoubtedly bound itself to the statement in the bills of lading in respect of the number of bags.

However, by mentioning the words 'said to weigh' and disclaiming that 'weight, contents and value when shipped (are) unknown', the carrier did not guarantee the weight particulars entered in the bills of lading. Thus, it was for the charterer-consignee to prove that the rice bags that were loaded at Bangkok were of the same weight as had been entered in the bills of lading. Only on providing such proof, could the charterer-consignee call upon the carrier to account for the shortage. Since such proof was not provided, the carrier was not liable for the alleged shortfall.

Shortage of Goods Received, Discharge Clauses, Pragmatic Interpretation

Title: General Traders Ltd *versus* Pierce Leslie (India) Ltd

Citation: ILR 1987 (1) Ker 237

Court: High Court of Kerala

Issue:

This was an appeal from the decree of a trial Court awarding the endorsee damages against the carrier for short landing of cargo. Amongst other points of the carrier's appeal, the pertinent one was that as the carrier, it had no responsibility for the goods after they had crossed the tackle of the ship. The pertinent issue before the Court was about the correct interpretation of the words 'discharge from the vessel'.

Facts:

SS Lucky Three was chartered to carry 15,000 bags of raw cashew nuts from Mombasa, Kenya, to Calicut, India, in January 1972. On arrival at Calicut, barges were arranged to transport the goods because Calicut was not a roadstead port and there was some distance between the piers and the nearest place where ships could reach. The lightering and barge transportation was conducted by the agent of the Charterer. It was at this stage that the goods were lost. Suit was filed on the basis of bills of lading that were issued by the master of *SS Lucky Three*. The carrier disclaimed responsibility by relying on a clause that stated, 'The carrier or his agent shall not be liable for loss or damage to the goods during the period before loading and after discharge from the vessel, howsoever such loss or damage arise'. They also relied on a clause that stated, 'Any lightering in or off ports of loading, or ports of discharge, has to be in the account of the merchant'.

However, another clause of the bill of lading provided that 'Loading, discharging and delivery of the cargo shall *be arranged by the Carriers' agent* unless otherwise agreed.....The merchant or his assign shall take delivery of the goods as fast as the vessel can deliver..... but only if required by the Carrier...'. Additionally, a clause in the introductory portion of the bill of lading stated that 'carriage to Calicut or so near thereto, as the vessel may safely get and lie always afloat, which *are to be delivered in the like good order and condition* at the aforesaid port unto the order, or to his or their assigns'.

Analysis:

The Court observed that it would be a preposterous result if a literal interpretation of the words 'discharge from the vessel' was taken to be correct. Such an interpretation would lead to meaningless results such as the exoneration of the carrier in the case of discharge at high seas. The intention behind these words had to be the delivery of goods to the endorsee. Until the endorsee is not in a position to take delivery of the goods, discharge from the ship cannot be said to have been complete. The term 'discharge from the vessel', unless the contract otherwise indicates, would mean effective and actual discharge in a reasonable manner that enables the endorsee to take delivery of the goods.

Thus, in a non-roadstead port like Calicut, where transhipment of the cargo from the ship to the pier was inevitable, and lightering was a normal course of action for unloading the cargo on the shore, the endorsee could not be understood to be taking delivery at anchorage.

The words 'discharge from the vessel' were given a pragmatic interpretation to mean that the goods were to be discharged from the vessel in such a condition that the endorsee can take effective delivery of the goods. The Court noted that the law on this point was clear, the carrier's responsibility continues till the time the cargo is unloaded on the shore, unless something else is specifically mentioned in the contract. The Court dismissed the carrier's appeal.

Damaged Cargo, Role of Inspection, Material Difference

Title: SGS India Ltd *versus* Dolphin International Ltd

Citation: 2021 SCC Online SC 879

Court: Supreme Court of India

Issue:

This was an appeal from a judgment of the National Consumer Disputes Redressal Commission (NCDRC) that granted the shipper a decree against the testing, inspection, and certification company, that inspected the shipper's cargo during loading. The pertinent issue before the Court was whether the inspection company was responsible for the mismatch in specifications between the inspection certificate and those found at the port of discharge?

Facts:

The shipper contracted with the inspection company to inspect the groundnut that the shipper was transporting to Greece and the Netherlands. The groundnuts were inspected prior to loading and inspection certificates were issued. On reaching their ports of destination, the groundnuts were inspected and disputes about the size of the groundnuts at Greece, and the levels of Aflatoxin at Netherlands, were raised. The shipper argued that the inspection company was liable for the difference in specification found at the ports of discharge. Since the inspection company was not able to show that extraneous factors during the voyage could have affected the cargo, the NCDRC held them liable.

Analysis:

An inspection company is not responsible for what happens to the cargo during the voyage. It is the responsibility of the shipper, as the party complaining, to show that there was negligent and deficient service by the inspection company in performing their obligations. The shipper had not escaped this burden.

It was not the inspection company's contractual obligation to ensure that the goods were of the same specifications at ports of loading and discharge. The inspection certificates also clearly disclaimed responsibility for differing Aflatoxin levels. In any case, the shipper could not even prove that the samples retained by the inspection company were materially different in respect of their specifications from the inspection reports. A deficiency of service claim could have only been maintained if the shipper could prove that the inspection certificates and the samples sent to the shipper afterwards were materially different.

Wrong Goods, Nature Unknown, Non-Admiralty Breach

Title: National Co Ltd *versus* MS Asia Mariner

Citation: Admiralty Suit No 01 of 1967

Court: High Court of Calcutta

Issue:

This was an application for dismissal of suit and release of a ship under arrest. The shipowner had pleaded that there was no breach of the contract of carriage and hence, the vessel should be released. The pertinent issue was whether the misstatement of the carried goods on the bills of lading tantamounted to a breach of the contract of carriage.

Facts:

The ship, *MS Asia Mariner*, was chartered by the seller for a voyage from Bangkok, Thailand, to Calcutta, India, to deliver 1000 tons of Grade–C, Thai (Mesta) Jute, of the crop of 1966-67. The seller was paid under a letter of credit scheme. When the cargo reached Calcutta, it was found that the 1000 tons of jute were not 'Grade–C, Thai (Mesta) Jute, of the crop of 1966-67' but was 'Jute cutting'. The bills of lading stated that the goods were 'Siam Mesta Jute, Grade - C' and that 'contents, nature, quality, measure, weight, marks, numbers and value (were) unknown'. The consignee refused to take delivery on the basis that these were not the goods mentioned on the bills of lading. The consignee alleged that the shipowner had knowingly misstated the goods on the bills of lading to allow the seller to benefit from the letter of credit scheme. The shipowner contended that it was not liable for breach of the contract of carriage because it had delivered the goods which it had received for shipment.

Analysis:

Words on the bills of lading must reflect actual events that they purport to evidence. In this case, the bills of lading stated that the shipowner shall only be liable for damage or loss arising from breach or non-performance of an obligation of the contract of carriage. Therefore, the Court had to identify what were the obligations upon the shipowner emanating from the contract of carriage of goods.

Carriage of goods meant carriage of goods actually shipped and not hypothetical goods which were never shipped. This was not a case of the shipped goods being undelivered, short delivered, delayed or damaged. Furthermore, the words of the bills of lading made it clear that the shipowner was not aware of the contents of the cargo. This was reflected in its disclaimer and also in the fact that the type of jute was only mentioned under the column 'shipper's particulars'. The shipowner could not be held responsible for the goods which had never been given to it i.e. those which were never shipped.

The contravention of the Hague Rules in issuing the bills of lading was not a breach of the contract of carriage of goods. The consignee may have had a case against the shipowner for not stating the correct type of jute if they knew or ought to have known what the goods were. Misstatements made in bills of lading precede their transformation into contracts of carriage when they are delivered to the consignee. The misstatements do not constitute a breach of the contract of carriage. They can possibly be a separate and distinct breach. However, that is not a case which can attract the arresting powers of a Court in its Admiralty Jurisdiction. The Court accepted the application and released the ship.

Damaged Cargo, Incorporation Clause, Intent

Title: MV Baltic Confidence *versus* State of Trading Corporation of India Ltd

Citation: AIR 2001 SC 3381

Court: Supreme Court of India

Issue:

This was an appeal from an order of the High Court of Calcutta that dismissed the shipowner's application to refer the matter to arbitration. The Court was to assess whether the arbitration clause of the charterparty was properly incorporated into the bills of lading. The pertinent question before the Court was whether the parties to the bills of lading, one of whom was not a party to the formation of the charterparty, intended that the arbitration clause be incorporated?

Facts:

The ship, *MV Baltic Confidence*, was chartered in May 1997, for transporting yellow peas from Vancouver, Canada, to Calcutta, India. Part of the cargo was found to be damaged by seawater when it was received by the consignee. The consignee filed a suit against the shipowner, who had issued the bills of lading, and the time charterer, for failure to deliver the goods in good order and condition. Cl 1 of the 'Conditions of Carriage' of the bills, the incorporation clause, stated that 'All terms and conditions, liberties and exceptions of the Charter Party, dated as overleaf, including the

Law and Arbitration Clause, are herewith incorporated'. The related charterparty clause started with the words 'this charterparty shall be governed...'.

Analysis:

After considering a number of cases from the United Kingdom and India, the Court decided to reconstruct the intent of the parties as it would have been at the time of the formation of the contracts of carriage i.e. the bills of lading. It held that the incorporation clause should be given meaning and effect, instead of frustrating or invalidating it by reading it literally, pedantically and technically. If on the construction of the charterparty clause, no absurd, insensible, or inconsistent effect is noticed, then the clause should be made binding on the parties to the bill of lading. The clause did not give rise to such an effect.

The parties had knowledge of the charterparty clause, and they had chosen to specifically incorporate it into the bills of lading. This made it clear that they had intended for an arbitrator to resolve their disputes. The parties had taken care not to couch the incorporation clause in general terms by using the expression 'including the Law and Arbitration clause'. This was a specific reference. The fact, that the charterparty clause started with the words 'this charterparty' and not 'this bill of lading', did not make it inoperative in the contractual relationship of the consignee and the shipowner, because the intention of the parties was to apply it to the bills of lading.

Rejected Goods, Agent's Negligence, Frustration of Remedy

Title: Penguin Maritime Ltd *versus* Lee & Muirhead Ltd

Citation: 2014 SCC Online Bom 994

Court: High Court of Bombay

Issue:

This was a suit filed by the shipowner against its port agent for acting without authorisation and in conflict with the shipowner's interest. The pertinent issue before the Court was whether the port agent had acted negligently in giving an undertaking to the port that the ship will provide clean mate's receipts for the cargo that was to be loaded.

Facts:

The vessel, *MV Lissom*, was chartered to transport rice from Haldia, West Bengal, India, in 1996. As was customary and possibly convenient, a common port agent was appointed to look after the affairs of the shipowner, the charterer, and the shipper at the port of loading. For the shipowner, the port agent's express obligation was to ensure that the cargo was ready for loading when the ship arrived and to appoint a surveyor to check the quality of the cargo prior to loading. When the ship arrived, the cargo was not ready for loading nor had it been surveyed. On surveying, it was found that the cargo of rice was unsuitable for human consumption because it was infested with insects, weevils, and larvae. This would have been an obvious case of rejection of cargo or issuing qualified bills of lading, if it were not for the port agent. The port agent had not informed the shipowner that a bylaw of the port required that only clean receipts be issued for the goods shipped from the port, or the goods be rejected or returned, if they were before shipment or after shipment, respectively. Alternatively, the bylaw stated that if a qualified receipt was issued then this be counter signed by the shipper. Additionally, the port agent had given an undertaking, unbeknown to the shipowner, to the port authority that the cargo was already available for loading at the port and that clean bills of lading, in their respect, would be issued by the shipowner. On knowledge of this fact, the shipowner chose to sue the port agent, instead of the charterer and the shipper, for its losses.

Analysis:

An agent must act in the best interest of their principal. They cannot impose upon their principal what is best for them. A clean bill of lading for damaged goods would lead to the presumption that goods were damaged in transit and that would expose the shipowner to liability.

In this case, the port agent was acting for the shipowner but also for the charterer and the shipper. The shipper had provided cargo that was not entitled to a clean bill of lading or mate's receipt, given the cargo's obvious faults. By exercising honesty, the agent could have asked the shipper to provide clean cargo. Instead, they chose to demand a clean bill of lading from the shipowner. The events that followed led to delays and expenses, for which the shipowner rightfully held the agent responsible.

The port agent's interpretation that the bylaw mandated that a clean bill of lading be issued for any quality of goods, was wrong. The bylaw had a provision for rejection and return of unclean goods. However, the port agent's undertaking to the port authority, that clean bills of lading will be issued, took away the shipowner's right of rejection. The knowledge of this bylaw could not be imputed to a foreign principal who had hired the port agent to look after their affairs in that port. It was the responsibility of the agent to inform the shipowner of this bylaw. Crucially, the bylaw also had a spatial element where it differentiated between the place of loading and the place of sorting of the goods. It was the agent's responsibility to ensure that the goods which were sent to the place of loading had been surveyed for quality.

Correspondingly, the port agent had wrongfully stated, to the port authority, that the goods were already available for loading. As the facts showed, neither were they at the port nor had they been surveyed. The effect of the agent's statement was that it implied that the goods had been surveyed and found to be in apparent good order and condition. It, therefore, implied that a clean bill of lading would be issued by the shipowner. Since these acts were done on behalf of the shipowner, they prevented the shipowner from claiming against the charterer and the shipper. It also placed the shipowner in a precarious situation where, if they transported the goods, they would have been exposed to a claim for damage to, precisely, those goods from the consignee. The shipowner was correct in holding the port agent liable for the losses they had suffered due to the agent's neglect in performing their obligations.

Shortage and Damage to Goods Received, Clean Bill of Lading, Balance of Evidence

Title: Jayanti Shipping Co Ltd *versus* The Food Corporation of India

Citation: 1979 SCC Online Ker 191

Court: High Court of Kerala

Issue:

This was an appeal by the shipowner against an order of a trial Court allowing the claim of the bill of lading holder for short landed and damaged cargo. The pertinent issues at this appeal were: whether the bill of lading had been properly endorsed? What was the evidentiary value of the bill of lading? Were the survey reports valid evidence? Where did the responsibility of the shipowner end vis-à-vis in discharging the cargo?

Facts:

The bill of lading holder was to receive a cargo of bags of Thailand White Rice being transported by the ship, *SS Ramajayanthi*, from Bangkok, Thailand, to Cochin, India, in 1968. The discharge was conducted by landing agents at the port. There was a shortfall of several bags, several other bags were torn, cut and slack, and others were contaminated by Sulphur, allegedly emanating from the holds of the ship. The bill of lading holder sued the shipowner on the basis of the clean and unqualified bills of lading. The shipowner argued that the bills of lading were mere receipts because they had been issued pursuant to a charterparty. Therefore, they did not represent an admission on behalf of the shipowner in respect of their contents and/or quality. Notably, the Government of India was the charterer of the ship and both, the bill of lading holder and the shipowner, were government companies.

Analysis:

Endorsement of a bill of lading transfers with it the rights and title to the goods. The shipowner argued that the bill of lading holder was unable to show that it was the full owner of the goods or that the goods had been endorsed to it with intent to transfer the full title over the goods. However, a clause in the charterparty transferred the rights and liabilities of the charterer to the bill of lading holder. Additionally, the shipowner had possession of the original bills of lading and had failed to present them in Court. This took away the strength of their argument that there was 'no valid endorsement on the bills of lading'. There was also evidence to show that the shipowner treated the bill of lading holder as the party entitled to the cargo: an invoice in relation to the cargo was addressed to it, the certificate of discharge was countersigned by its officer, the port's outturn statement was issued to it, and there was evidence of communication from the shipowner to the bill of lading holder where no doubts were raised in respect of its competency. The trial Court was right in holding the bill of lading holder entitled to sue.

A clause in the charterparty stated that bills of lading will be conclusive evidence against the shipowner of the number of bags. Another clause stated that the shipowner will take all necessary steps to prevent contamination of rice cargo by contact with other types of cargo. This, combined with the effect of judicial precedents in relation to clean bills of lading which estopped the shipowner from claiming the lack of apparent good order and condition, gave the bill of lading holder a valid cause of action.

The shortfall was proved by the count of bags shown in the outturn statement issued by the port. Additionally, the cargo collected through sweeping amounted to a substantial number of bags. Additionally, a survey was commissioned by the bill of lading holder with due intimation to the shipowner and its agent. This survey showed that several of the offloaded bags were torn, cut, and slack. It also showed that several of them had been contaminated by Sulphur. No dispute was raised to the qualification, competency, and neutrality of the surveyors by the shipowner. There was no reason why this evidence could not be accepted as correct and reliable to prove the bill of lading holder's claim.

The shipowner argued that it was absolved of liability post the cargo leaving the ship's tackles into the possession of the landing agents. The nature of the role of landing agents was that they acted as intermediaries in their duties to both parties. However, before the bill of lading was exhausted, the agent was acting for the shipowner. They become agents of the endorsee on presentation of the bills of lading and delivery order. This meant that the goods had to be put into the dominion and control of the endorsee by the shipowner or its agent.

Shortage of Goods Received, Unattended Arbitration Notice, Effect of Silence and Inaction

Title: Food Corporation of India *versus* Thakur Shipping Co

Citation: AIR 1975 SC 469

Court: Supreme Court of India

Issue:

This was an appeal by the charterer against a High Court order that allowed the shipowner's application for stay of judicial proceedings. The pertinent issue was whether silence and inaction of the shipowner to repeated letters of the charterer indicated their unwillingness to proceed with arbitration. The answer to this issue would have clarified whether the charterer's recourse to judicial proceedings was valid.

Facts:

Two ships were chartered for carriage of rice from Thailand to India by the same charterer. Consequently, two similar charterparty(s) were also executed. Both charterparty(s) contained the same arbitration clause. The bills of lading issued in pursuance of the charters contained a time bar provision which barred any suits from being maintained after one year of the date on which the ship arrived at the port of discharge. At the same time, the bills of lading also incorporated the Indian Carriage of Goods by Sea Act, 1925, which stated that the time bar starts one year from the date of delivery. Both ships discharged their cargo at the port of discharge. The charterer found that the cargo was short delivered from both ships and raised claims with agents of both shipowners. In both cases, the shipowners chose to remain silent and did not respond to the charterer's letters.

Thereafter, the charterer instituted suits against both shipowners. Both shipowners, on receiving Court summons, responded with applications to stay the judicial proceedings in light of the arbitration clause in the charterparty(s) stating that they were ready and willing to arbitrate.

Analysis:

A judicial body ordinarily requires parties to a contract to resort, for resolving disputes arising under a contract, to the tribunal contemplated by them at the time of the formation of the contract.

The trial Court found that the shipowners took no steps to refer the dispute to arbitration in spite of being urged to do so by the charterer. This fact led the trial Court to conclude that the shipowners were not ready and willing to go to arbitration. They were only waiting for the claim to be barred by lapse of time.

The shipowners had to show that they were ready and willing to proceed to arbitration for their stay applications to be granted. In this case, however, they had chosen to stay silent and such conduct could not be defended as being 'mere inaction' incapable of colouring their 'readiness and willingness'. Failing to act, when they were called upon to do so, was a positive gesture signifying unwillingness and/or want of readiness to go to arbitration.

The shipowners could not argue that their readiness and willingness to arbitrate should be judged from the moment their applications were filed. There were judicial precedents which stated that readiness and willingness to arbitrate must exist at the commencement of the legal proceedings and not only when an application for stay is made.

Also, the shipowners could not use the excuse that the charterer had, in one of its letters, deviated from the arbitration clause. If the shipowners were ready and willing to arbitrate, they should have replied to the letter instead of relying on it to deny doing anything for the proper conduct of the arbitration. Their silence and inaction justified the conclusion that they were not ready or willing.

Rejected Goods, Deviation, Intervening Acts

Title: Priyanka Overseas Pvt Ltd *versus* Joongang Shipping Co Ltd

Citation: [2018] OMP 378/2008

Court: High Court of Delhi

Issue:

This was a challenge to an arbitral award holding, mostly, in favour of the shipowner. The issue was whether the calculation of deviation days occasioned by the charterer's fault did not account for reasonable voyage time. The pertinent issue was whether the shipowner's actions had elongated the deviation beyond the reasonable voyage time.

Facts:

In 2001, the chartered ship proceeded from Kandla, India, to Umm Qasr, Iraq, to deliver wheat. On inspection at Umm Qasr, the buyer rejected the wheat. The charterer then found another buyer in Hodeidah, Yemen. The voyage from Umm Qasr to Hodeidah took a little over 28 days. The charterer and shipowner raised claims against each other that included claims for the deviation and bunker costs from Umm Qasr to Hodeidah. At arbitration, the charterer was held responsible for initiating the deviation from Umm Qasr. Consequently, in determining the amount of damages to be paid for the said deviation, the tribunal calculated on the basis of total days (28-29) taken to reach Hodeidah from Umm Qasr. The charterer disputed this calculation on the ground that the deviation took more than the reasonable voyage time (7-8 days) because of the shipowner's actions. The shipowner had waited at Khorfakkan Anchorage, Fuzairah, the United Arab Emirates, for receipt of a Letter of Indemnity (LoI) from the Charterer.

Analysis:

The initiator of a general deviation will not suffer harm caused due to the other party's intervening actions.

It was untenable that, although the tribunal found that the shipowner took an unreasonably long time to reach Hodeidah yet, it awarded charges for the entirety of the period. The time taken could also not be justified by the shipowner by way of reasoning. The Court noted that the arbitral tribunal had recorded the shipowner's reasons 'lack of conviction and proper justification'. The arbitral tribunal's findings in respect of the shipowner's actions and calculation of the number of days of deviation were contradictory. The arbitral tribunal had observed that the shipowner 'could have, and should have' continued the voyage instead of waiting at Fuzairah. This should have led to the inescapable conclusion that the charterer was not to be made liable for the actions of the shipowner. The charterer's challenge was accepted.

Delayed Delivery, Foreseeable Losses, Information

Title: MV Quang Minh 126 *versus* Bohra Industries Ltd

Citation: 2010 SCC Online Guj 3217

Court: High Court of Gujarat

Issue:

This was an application for vacating arrest filed by the shipowner. The issue before the Court was whether, on prima facie examination, a case of breach of charterparty had been made? The pertinent issue was whether the losses claimed, as a consequence of the breach, were known or foreseeable by the shipowner?

Facts:

In December 2009, the charterer hired the *MV Quang Minh 126* to bring a cargo of Phosphate in rock form from Hai Phong, Vietnam, to Kandla, India. The charterparty mentioned the window of days between which loading was to be done at Vietnam. It did not mention when the vessel was to be expected in India. As it turned out, the vessel reached India 25-28 days beyond the expectation of the charterer. Eventually, the charterer made a claim for consequential losses and arrested the vessel. They substantiated their claim for consequential losses by arguing that the cargo was required for manufacturing a product which was to be sold onwards. Additionally, that their factory had been idle. They argued that since the shipowner was aware of the nature of their business, they ought to have known of these consequences.

In this application to vacate the order of arrest, the shipowner argued that the charterer's claims were remote and indirect. They argued that the possibility of these losses were never informed to the shipowner at the time of formation of the charterparty.

Analysis:

If time is of essence, a relevant stipulation must be stated in the charterparty. In the present case, there was no stipulation in the charterparty that the vessel should reach Kandla on or before a particular date. Thus, the Court could not conclude that an express term of the contract had been breached. The charterer had also not informed the shipowner, at the time of formation of the charterparty, that there were onward sale contracts for the manufactured product which required this cargo to be delivered on time. The applicable provision of the statute on contract law, and judicial precedent, only allowed for losses which naturally arose in the usual course of business from the breach or were known to the shipowner. Since the shipowner was not informed by the Charterer of the onward sale contracts, the shipowner could not be held liable.

The fact, that the charterer was not able to provide evidence of these onward sale contracts, also invalidated their claim. They could neither prove loss of profit nor liability from onward buyers. It was also telling that the charterer had withdrawn the claims for loss of goodwill and difference in price of Sulphuric Acid (an ingredient in the manufacturing process). The Court took this as evidence of the conduct of the charterer in making huge and exaggerated claims.

The only claims which seemed plausible at this prima facie stage was that for idling factory time and loss of interest on freight payment. The arrest was maintained for solely these two claims.

Damaged Goods, Applicable Law, Intent

Title: Indian Shipping Industry Ltd *versus* Dominion of India

Citation: AIR 1953 BOM 396

Court: High Court of Bombay

Issue:

This was an application by the shipper to decide preliminary issues, in a suit filed by the shipowner to recover money. The issue before the Court was whether the shipowner was under an absolute obligation to provide a seaworthy vessel? The pertinent question was whether the contract between the parties was a contract of carriage by sea to which the domestic law applied?

Facts:

In January 1944, the shipowner entered into a contract of affreightment with the shipper to transport cloth from Bombay, India, to Cochin and Allepey, India. The contract did not provide that any particular vessel had to be used. The vessel that was eventually employed, *Jayant*, could not make it much further than Bombay. The cargo was damaged due to water ingress. Consequently, the shipper claimed its right to the security deposit of the shipowner. The shipowner, on the other hand, filed this suit for return of the security deposit as well as freight payment and other expenses. The shipowner argued that the contract was governed by the domestic law of carriage and therefore, there was no absolute obligation on them to provide a seaworthy vessel. The shipper argued that the domestic law did not apply, and the shipowner could not escape their obligation to provide a seaworthy vessel.

Analysis:

The main point of contention between the two parties was whether the contract of affreightment satisfied the definition of 'contract of carriage'. The answer to this question would determine whether the domestic law applied and thus, whether there was an absolute obligation to provide a seaworthy vessel.

The domestic law disallowed implying seaworthiness obligations. The definition of 'contract of carriage' was:

> applies only to contracts of carriage covered by a bill of lading or any similar document of title, in so far as such document relates to the carriage of goods by sea including any bill of lading or any similar document as aforesaid issued under or pursuant to a charterparty from the moment at which such bill of lading or similar document of title regulates the relations between a carrier and a holder of the same.

First, the Court analysed the nature of the contract. They found that the contract did not specify the name of the ship and none of the terms revealed the identity of the ship. The contract, in fact, stated that a 'country craft' was to be provided by the shipowner. The shipowner could have provided any country craft. In light of this, the Court held that it was impossible to call the contract a charterparty, which is a contract to hire a specific ship.

Next, the Court had to determine the meaning of the words 'covered by a bill of lading'. They held that these words did not mean that the contract is actually covered by such a bill. They reflected the need for intent of deliverance of the bill of lading. As the evidence had shown, there were clear indications of intent to receive a bill of lading by the shipper. Not only had the shipper instructed the shipowner to issue bills of lading when it loaded the cargo, but the shipper also required that duplicate bills of lading be annexed to the invoices for freight payment. There was also evidence to show that the shipper had actually negotiated on the proper form of the bills of lading. Additionally, a letter from the shipper had complained about lack of information on the bills of lading. The Court held that this was a contract of carriage covered by a bill of lading and therefore, the domestic law applied.

The next contention which the Court had to deal with was the shipper's argument that the words 'from the moment...' applied to all the bills of lading and not just the bills of lading issued pursuant to charterparty contracts. The Court highlighted that there are several different ways of forming, and manifestations of, contracts of carriage. Where there was no charterparty and the shipper obtained a bill of lading, it became a repository of rights. This bill of lading became effective when it was given to the shipper by the shipowner. This position was different from cases of charterparty contracts because there the bill of lading regulates the relationship of parties during a different period of time than the charterparty. It was also telling that the plain grammatical construction of the definition was incompatible with the shipper's interpretation.

Misdelivery, Bills of Lading, Agent's Responsibility

Title: Shaw Wallace & Co Ltd *versus* Nepal Food Corporation

Citation: 2011 (15) SCC 56

Court: Supreme Court of India

Issue:

This was an appeal challenging two orders of a division bench of a High Court that upheld two decrees against the shipowner's agent. The issue was whether the agent was responsible for issuing bills of lading to the shipper on receiving the mate's receipts? The pertinent issue was whether there was a statutory duty upon the agent to do so even in light of the shipowner's clear instructions not to?

Facts:

Sometime in late 1978, two vessels, *MV Pichit Samut* and *MV Eastern Grand*, were chartered by a buyer to bring rice from Calcutta, India, to Penang, Malaysia, from the same shipper. The transactions were covered by separate letters of credit that had a period of validity after which they expired.

For both the cases, the shipowner's agent was the same. Both vessels suffered delays due to insufficient quantity of cargo at the time of loading. The agent was instructed not to issue bills of lading to the shipper till the shipper issued bank guarantees for the demurrage charges in both the cases. The shipper was issued mate's receipts as and when cargo was loaded onto the vessels. In the case of *MV Pichit Samut*, the shipper immediately circulated the mate's receipt to the shipowner's agent for release of the bills of lading. In the case of *MV Eastern Grand*, the shipper did not do so till the period of validity of the letter of credit had expired. The vessels delivered the cargo at Penang without receiving the bills of lading. Since the bills of lading were not delivered to the shipper, they could not enforce the letters of credit prior to their expiry. Additionally, the buyer was wound up and so the shipper was left without any remedy against them.

The shipper filed two suits against the shipowner and their agent for wrongful delivery and failure to furnish bills of lading. In both the cases, the shipper argued that the shipowner's agent was duty bound to furnish the bills of lading on time so that the shipper could benefit from the letters of credit. The agent argued that it was not bound to do so because it had clear instructions from the shipowner not to. The single judge and the division bench of the High Court held in favour of the shipper. They found that the agent had committed conversion by violating their statutory duty to issue the bills and their legal duty to deliver the bills to the shipper when demanded.

Analysis:

After receipt of cargo, the shipowner's agent is dutybound to deliver to the shipper the bills of lading pertaining to the received cargo.

The agent's argument that they were not liable because they were acting on behalf of the shipowner was not accepted. This was because the agent had a statutory duty to issue the bills of lading when the shipper demanded. The customary practice was for the shipper to receive a mate's receipt from the master at the time of loading which, when presented to the shipowner or their agent, was to entitle the shipper to the bill of lading. This, in fact, was done by the shipper but the shipowner's agent had refused to issue the bill of lading citing written instructions from the shipowner.

Crucially, the shipper not being the charterer, was not liable to the shipowner for claims regarding the operation of the ship such as the demurrage claimed in this case. By withholding the bills of lading, the shipowner's agent had obfuscated an innocent party's right. The agent should have realised that the mate's receipt represented the authority and instruction to issue the bills of lading to the shipper. The likelihood of a dispute between the shipper and buyer, in respect of a payment to the shipowner by the buyer, was not a sufficient reason to suspend the authorisation present in the mate's receipt.

The agent's actions were deliberate by their own admission of adhering to their principal's (the shipowner) instructions. They additionally amounted to negligent actions. This gave rise to the shipper's right to claim damages. The agent's argument that it was always the master of the ship who was responsible for issuing the bills of lading fell flat in light of well recognised practices, and the agent's own actions showing apparent authority. The agent had represented themselves as the agent of the shipowner and done all acts expected of them. They executed all the documentation and correspondence with the shipper's agent. Eventually, they were the ones who issued the bills of lading. All these acts showed that they were responsible for the issuance of the bills. Even after the mate's receipts had been received by them, and the shipper had notified them of their expectation of the bills, the agent never informed the shipper that they were not responsible for the bills.

The agent was, therefore, jointly and severally liable, along with the shipowner for the shipper's losses.

However, in the case of the *MV Pichit Samut*, the shipper had demanded issuance of bills of lading well within the period of validity of the letters of credit. Interestingly, in the case of the *MV Eastern Grand*, they had not done so till after the expiry of the letters of credit. The single judge was incorrect to find in favour of the shipper's argument that they had raised oral demands for the bills prior to the expiry date. None of the evidence on record evinced support for such an argument. This meant that in one case the agent was indeed liable for the loss to the shipper but, in the other case, they were not.

Mainly Relating to Documents

Demurrage, Nature of Clause, Intention and Understanding

Title: Ultratech Cement Ltd *versus* Sunfield Resources Pty Ltd

Citation: 2016 SCC Online Bom 10023

Court: High Court of Bombay

Issue:

This was an appeal from the judgment of a single judge bench affirming the order of dismissal by an arbitrator in a dispute relating to the effect of a demurrage clause in an international sale of goods contract. The buyer's arguments, that the demurrage clause was in the nature of an indemnity, and that the demurrage amount was in the nature of liquidated damages, were denied in both the previous stages. The pertinent issue in this appeal was whether, on the proper construction of the clause, the parties had absolutely agreed to the amount mentioned? In other words, was the amount in the nature of a fixed charge?

Facts:

The buyer and seller entered into a contract for bulk steaming non-coking coal in 1999. The contract provided for delivery of the cargo in batches, of which five batches were firm orders and one was optional. The demurrage clause stated that 'At the discharging port, buyers shall pay demurrage to the Seller or Vessel owners through sellers *if* required...'. The firm cargo was subsequently nominated and shipped from Richards Bay, South Africa, to Pipavav and Chennai, India. On each of the discharges, a 'statement of facts' was signed by the Master of the vessel, the vessel's agent, and the buyer's agent. On the basis of these documents, the seller raised invoices on the buyer for demurrage.

Analysis:

It was not in dispute that the vessels went on demurrage. It was only pertinent to decide what was the consequence of the demurrage clause. In this context, it became necessary to consider the purport of the clause which was to be decided on the basis of the meaning, intention, and commercial understanding, that the parties to the contract attributed to the clause at the time of the formation of the contract.

The buyer's argument that their liability to pay was dependent on the seller first paying demurrage to the vessel owner(s) was not reflected in the clause in any manner. The buyer's argument was an attempt to create an unwarranted confusion. Furthermore, there was fatal evidence to the buyer's claim by their employee that previous payments in similar contracts were made on the basis of three documents: (i) statement of facts given by the seller, (ii) verification thereof and if necessary, correction thereto, and (iii) the charterparty contract. Thus, the parties had commercially positioned themselves in a way which did not support the argument that the clause was in the nature of an indemnity.

However, the buyer's main argument on this appeal was, that the payment of demurrage charges was in the nature of liquidated damages, and that these were needed to be proved prior to payment. For this, the parties' commercial understanding during the time of the formation of the contract was required to be decoded. This would clarify how the parties understood the demurrage clause in the working of the contract. Prior correspondence showed that the demurrage/despatch rate was specifically agreed. In fact, it was the buyer who had specifically asked for the rates prior to shipment. This showed their real understanding.

The fact that parties agreed to a specific amount in the contract was itself evidence of the measure of damages. The evidentiary value of the amount could have been displaced by showing evidence of its unreasonableness or excessiveness. However, when parties, who were experts in the field of their transaction, agreed to a specific amount, by application of their commercial wisdom, the burden of proof was on the party claiming that the agreed amount was unreasonable. Otherwise, the agreed amount was to be considered a genuine pre-estimate of damages.

The buyer had not claimed that the charges were unreasonable or excessive. They did not even dispute the occurrence of the demurrage event. Additionally, the Court was inclined to believe that the demurrage charge represented a genuine pre-estimate of damages because of the peculiarity of shipping contracts. Several elements of international commerce and trade made it unreasonable, unrealistic, and impossible, to ask for proof of damage. The purpose of agreeing to the demurrage charge was to avoid litigation and complexity in assessing damages in such situations. The demurrage clause was very clear in evidencing the parties' agreement on this issue. It was unfortunate that the buyer had still chosen to deprive the seller of the legitimate dues. The seller's claim was affirmed.

Charterparty Repudiation, Broker's Letter of Guarantee, Knowledge of Obligation

Title: POL India Projects Ltd *versus* Aurelia Reederei Eugen Friederich GmbH Schiffahrtsgesellschaft & Company KG

Citation: 2015 SCC Online Bom 1109

Court: High Court of Bombay

Issue:

This was an appeal from an arbitration award that held the charterer's broker liable to pay, under a letter of guarantee, for the charterer's failure to pay the shipowner. It was the contention of the broker that they were undertaking the usual obligations which applied to their role and those obligations did not include a guarantee. The pertinent issue before this Court, on appeal, was whether there was a valid contract of guarantee between the parties so as to establish the broker's liability. A subsidiary issue was whether the charterparty arbitration clause was incorporated into the contract by virtue of the words, 'This letter of guarantee of performance is issued without prejudice and carries with it all the rights, liabilities and exceptions of the said charter party'.

Facts:

In furtherance to a GENCON voyage charterparty made in 2008, the broker of the charterer issued a letter to the shipowner 'guaranteeing the performance of the voyage'. The charterer did not, eventually, perform the voyage.

The broker contended that they had only acted in a manner natural to the role of the broker which was to convey that the charterer will perform as agreed. A corollary, the broker argued, that it was not party to the charterparty contract.

The arbitral tribunal found that the broker had acted as the manager of the charterer and that its role as a guarantor was in addition to its role as a broker. In accepting that role, the broker accepted different responsibilities and liabilities than those of a broker. The tribunal also found that the letter of guarantee validly incorporated the charterparty arbitration clause.

Analysis:

The broker played a major role for the charterer. They were also fully aware of the charterparty terms. Although the broker did not sign the charterparty, they did sign a rider agreement. This rider agreement also made reference to the guarantee and included an arbitration clause. The guarantee was also mentioned in correspondence between the parties. The broker had also offered to provide the guarantee during negotiations of the charterparty. Thus, the broker was fully aware of the obligation they were undertaking as the guarantor. The guarantee was also executed in a manner that satisfied the procedure and requirements of the applicable law.

It was clear by reading the letter of guarantee that all terms of the charterparty, including the arbitration clause, were incorporated into the letter. The reference in a contract to a document, containing an arbitration clause, constitutes an arbitration agreement if the contract is in writing, and the reference is such as to make that arbitration clause part of the contract. Here, the broker's letter was a contract that referenced the charterparty document. The intent of the broker that the charterparty terms have contractual effect alongwith the guarantee was clear. The Court dismissed the broker's challenge and reaffirmed the broker's liability to pay as the guarantor.

Bunker Payment, Privity, Terms and Conduct

Title: Chemoil Adani Pvt Ltd *versus* MV Hansa Sonderburg

Citation: 2010 SCC Online Bom 647

Court: High Court of Bombay

Issue:

This was an appeal from an order of a single judge vacating the arrest of a ship. The pertinent issue was whether the contract for the supply of bunkers between a time charterer and the bunker supplier created privity with the ship and the demise charterer.

Facts:

An Indian bunker supplier had provided bunkers to the ship, *MV Hansa Sonderburg*. The contract to supply bunkers was made in June 2009 and the bunkers were supplied a month later. The demise charterer contended that the responsibility to make payment to the bunker supplier was that of the time charterer who had made the contract for its purchase. There were other documents which bore the signatures of one of the crew members; Master's Requisition, Landing Certificate, and Bunker Delivery Receipt, but they were post contractual documents that did not create the privity required at the time of formation of the contract. However, the Bunker Delivery Receipt incorporated cl 3(e) of the contract that sought to create privity.

The single judge held that, the signing of these documents did not affect the liability of the time charterer to the bunker supplier, as only they were bound by such documents. The judge, therefore, vacated the order of arrest.

Analysis:

The arrest could not have been vacated merely because there was no specific agreement between the supplier, the ship and the demise charterer.

The contract to supply bunkers stated that the bunkers were supplied to the 'credit of the vessel' as well as the buyer who was the time charterer here. Furthermore, there was a clause allowing the bunker supplier to exercise a maritime lien. The contract should have been perused carefully. It gave a very broad definition of 'buyer' and included the ship and the demise charterer. Clause 3 put the onus of notifying that a lien could not be created, on the buyer. This was not done. The contract stated that the Bunker Delivery Receipt was a material document evidencing the performance of the contract. These documents could not be termed as unilateral or self-serving. Whether the documents were post -contractual or post-performance was to be decided at the trial stage, much like the effect of the link between these documents and the contract.

Additionally, the fact that the contract was signed on a date earlier than the delivery did not create two separate or distinct contracts. The demise charterer's argument that the other documents were post-contractual and not a distinct contract was also indicative of the fact that they were not part of a separate contract. These complexities informed the Court's decision to hold, that any question of privity between the supplier, the ship and the demise charterer were to be assessed at the time of a proper trial. The Court, thus, held that the order to vacate arrest was invalid.

Demurrage, Exception of Restraints of Established Authorities, Effect of 'Without Fault'

Title: MMTC of India Ltd *versus* Interore Fertichem Resources SA

Citation: 2012 SCC Online Del 2497

Court: High Court of Delhi

Issue:

This was an appeal, filed by the buyer of goods against the order of a single judge who had set aside an arbitral award dismissing the seller's claim for demurrage. The issue was whether an exception of 'restraints of established authorities' to demurrage covered orders of judicial authorities in a civil suit? The pertinent issue in this respect was whether those orders arose 'without fault' of the buyer.

Facts:

In May 1999, an agreement for an international sale of urea in bulk was entered into. The seller chartered the vessel, *MV Sadan Kaptanoglu*, to transport the urea from Yuzhny, Ukraine, to Chennai, India.

As per the terms of the sale agreement, the seller and buyer were responsible for wharfage and demurrage charges resulting from their negligence, respectively. A force majeure clause included 'Acts of Government'. A bridge clause also imposed the conditions of the charterparty on both parties. This made the seller responsible for the load port and the buyer responsible for the discharge port. A clause also stipulated the discharge rate. On the other hand, a clause in the charterparty created an exception to liability for the charterer for a number of causes, including 'restraints of established authorities' and, extended the exception to any other cause which did not arise due to the fault of the charterer. Delays, giving rise to the demurrage claim, arose at the discharge port due to the buyer's disputes with their stevedores.

An arbitral tribunal in London, hearing the dispute between the shipowner and the charterer (also the seller), held the seller liable for the delays and thus, for demurrage. Pertinently, it did not agree with the defense, that the civil suit by the stevedores and the consequential events were 'restraints of established authorities'.

However, the arbitral tribunal that heard this dispute between the seller and the buyer agreed with that defense and favoured the buyer.

Analysis:

The force majeure clause of the sale agreement did not include 'acts of Courts'. However, there was judicial precedent which supported the buyer's argument that if they were not in control of an event, they could bring themselves within the relief of the force majeure clause. For this to happen, the buyer must show that the events were beyond their control.

When the first stevedore's contract was terminated, the buyer through their agent did not ascertain the quantity of the cargo, nor did they settle the first stevedore's accounts. If this was done, then the civil suit could have been avoided.

The exception clause of the charterparty was clear the charterer could not be held liable for events where they were not at fault. Non-avoidance of the civil-suit was treated as fault of the Charterer. Once this was clear, it was merely an exercise of shifting the Charterer's liability, from the seller to the buyer, by applying the clauses of their contract. If this was not done, then the effect would be to punish an innocent party, the seller, for the acts of the responsible party, the buyer. The buyer's appeal was dismissed.

Calculation of Laytime

Title: Jayshree Shipping *versus* Food Corporation of India Limited

Citation: 2008 Indlaw DEL 2183

Court: High Court of Delhi

Issue:

This was an appeal from an arbitral award that awarded the shipowner's claim for demurrage charges. The pertinent issue, was whether the effective date of the Notice of Readiness (NoR) was to be construed according to the charterparty or, was affected by the application of the Customs Act, 1962? The answer to this would have affected the start of laytime and which, in consequence, would have affected demurrage calculation. There was also the issue of what was the proper formula for calculating the duration of laytime.

Facts:

The vessel, *MV Jayalakshmi*, was chartered to carry grain from Austin, Texas, United States of America, to Nagapattinam, Tamil Nadu, India. After the charterparty was performed, disputes arose between the parties in respect of several heads of accounts. The arbitral tribunal found, that laytime started to count 24 hours after the NoR was tendered, because this was according to the charterparty. The charterer claimed that this finding did not consider the time taken by the Custom's Authorities to grant final entry. They claimed that the words 'also having entered at Custom House', appearing within the clause, mandated that the effective date of the NoR must be calculated after considering such time. They relied on two sections of the Customs Act, 1962, that related to the ship's duty to deliver an import manifest to the authorities, and a restriction on the ship from unloading goods prior to receipt of permission from the authorities, respectively.

The charterer also claimed that laytime calculation had been incorrectly done by the arbitral tribunal. They claimed that the tribunal should have calculated laytime on the basis of only 'workable' hatches. They also claimed, that 12 hours needed to be excluded from laytime calculation, on each of the discharging days, on account of the port's working hours.

Analysis:

There was judicial precedent which supported the interpretation, that time started running from the time of tender of NoR, and not from the time when the Custom's Authorities granted final entry. This was in line with shipping practice followed by the ports and customs officials in India. The charterparty clause had to be viewed from a commercial perspective. On doing so, there was nothing to restrict a plain and literal interpretation. The first requirement of laytime commencing after 24 hours of the Master tendering the NoR was an objective fact. The latter part of the clause, 'also having entered at Custom House', constituted a qualification of this objective fact. It was also true that the NoR was required to be submitted to the Custom's Authorities. In such a scenario, considering that the charterer was aware of these rules in the Customs Act, they should have incorporated a clear term in the charterparty, that the NoR would be considered effective from the date of acceptance by the Custom's Authorities. There being no such stipulation in the contract, the arbitral tribunal was well within their powers to come to a different interpretation.

The arbitral tribunal was also justified in applying the 'over-all rate' formula rather than the 'workable-hatch' formula, since the former had been accepted in a more recent judicial precedent.

Additionally, the arbitral tribunal was correct in ignoring the 12 hours during which the port was not working from the laytime calculation, because this was not a specified exclusion in the charterparty. The parties had specifically provided for other instances in the charterparty when time was not to count as laytime. Those clauses were detailed and exhaustive. The charterer should have, thus, included a stipulation for exclusion of time due to this eventuality in the charterparty.

Demurrage, Nature of Payment, Conduct

Title: Larsen and Toubro Ltd *versus* Sunfield Resources Pvt Ltd

Citation: 2005 (4) MhLJ 607

Court: High Court of Bombay

Issue:

This was a challenge to an arbitration award that gave the seller its claim for demurrage. The pertinent issue was whether the wording of the Contract of Affreightment (CoA), between the parties, made buyer's liability to pay demurrage dependant on the seller's payment to a third party (the shipowner)?

Facts:

Sometime in 1999, the buyer and seller entered into a contract for the sale of steaming coal through five necessary and one optional shipment. This CoA also had clauses on demurrage and despatch amongst other clauses relating to transportation. The steaming coal was transported to the buyer in India in five shipments. It was the claim of the seller that all five shipments had gone on demurrage, and that the buyer had failed to raise a dispute in respect of the demurrage claim as per the procedure provided by the CoA.

The buyer claimed that its liability to pay was dependant on the seller's payment to the shipowner i.e. that the nature of demurrage was that of indemnity. They also claimed that a 'strike' action had activated the force majeure clause which allowed them partial respite from demurrage calculation. They also counter claimed that the seller was in breach of not providing the sixth optional shipment. The demurrage/despatch clause which was at the centre of this dispute read as under:

10 (v) Demurrage/Despatch

At the discharging port, buyers shall pay demurrage to the Seller or Vessel owners, through sellers if required, at the rate not exceeding US$ 8000.00 per day or pro-rata for part of the day and seller shall pay despatch to buyers, if earned, at a rate of 50% of demurrage rate, not exceeding US$ 4000.00 per day or pro-rata for part of the day.

All demurrage or despatch to be settled within 60 days after laytime statement submitted with supporting documents, like Notices of Readiness, Statement of Facts and Time Sheets.

Any disagreement over the laytime statement must be raised by the other party within 30 days after such statement is transmitted and received, otherwise, the statement is accepted as correct.

Analysis:

The dispute between the parties hinged upon the use of the words 'if required' in the above clause. The buyer wanted this to be interpreted as an indemnity, whereas the seller advocated that the words did not affect the nature of demurrage at all. Since both gave differing interpretations, the arbitrator had to construe the meaning of the clause by studying the parties' conduct. The safest method to find out the correct meaning of the clause was to find out how the parties understood the clause. This could be deduced from their conduct when the contract was being performed.

It was fatal that the buyer had never raised the indemnity argument with the seller during the performance of the contract. Even after the seller had raised their claim for demurrage, the buyer did not ask for 'payment receipts'. These documents would have been relevant to any party claiming that their liability to pay was dependent on the seller's payment to the shipowner. These documents would have actually established that the seller made payment to the shipowner. Crucially, a witness who was the buyer's employee had given evidence that they only asked for the statement of fact (SoF), verification of the SoF, and the charterparty. These documents did not evidence actual payment by the seller to the shipowner. Quite opposite, the buyer's correspondence to the seller, after the demurrage claim had been raised, did not show any signs that they disagreed or disputed the claim. In their correspondence, the buyer did not even ask for a document that could indicate the buyer's reliance on the seller's payment to the shipowner. Had the buyer understood the clause to be an indemnity clause, they would have asked for a document that showed the amount of demurrage paid by the seller to the shipowner. By merely arguing the above, at the stage of arbitration, the buyer could not prove that their understanding of the clause was that it was in the nature of indemnity.

The buyer was liable to pay the demurrage claim of the seller because the seller had followed the contractual procedure stated in the second part of the above clause. The demurrage rate was informed to the buyer by the seller each time the nominated vessel arrived. The buyer raised no dispute. Subsequently, the seller incorporated the demurrage rate into its laytime statement. The buyer raised no dispute. The statements were submitted within the timeline prescribed by the above clause and the buyer did not raise any disputes. Therefore, the buyer's acceptance of the demurrage rate and their payment liability was unambiguous.

Although it was true that a force majeure clause prescribed relief from liability due to 'strike' action, it was the buyer's burden to prove that the delay was, solely or partly, because of the strike. The buyer had not done so.

As far as the buyer's counter-claim for the sixth optional cargo was concerned, it too failed because the buyer had not exercised the option within the time allocated by the CoA. Additionally, the letters that exercised this option were not addressed to the correct person, and they did not include language which could be understood to mean that the option was being exercised. The buyer's argument, that time was not of essence in exercising the options, was incorrect. Thus, the buyer's challenge was dismissed.

Demurrage, Exclusion Clauses, Interpretation

Title: Steel Authority of India Limited *versus* Mercator Lines Limited

Citation: (Lexis Nexis) IND 2012 BOM 951

Court: High Court of Bombay

Issue:

This was a challenge to an arbitration award which gave the shipowner their claim for demurrage. The pertinent issue was whether the charterer could rely on general exclusions after its reliance on specific exclusions had failed?

Facts:

In 2015, *MV Prem Poorva* was chartered to carry cargo from Hay Point, Queensland, Australia, to various ports in India. The vessel first visited Vishakhapatnam and then Haldia. The parties went to arbitration on the question of demurrage payment. In the arbitration, the charterer claimed that the delay was caused because one of the cranes of the ship was not functioning, and that this was the reason that the port authorities had prevented it from discharging. The charterer had contended that this eventuality was specifically excluded as per the terms of the charterparty. The arbitrator found that the ship had been able to discharge, at the agreed discharge rate, despite one crane not functioning. The charterer could, therefore, not rely on the specific exclusion.

Then in the Court, the charterer tried to bring their case within the general exclusion clause. The relevant part of this clause stated that:

> 42. At the discharge port, time lost by reason of all or any of following causes shall not to be counted as discharge time, unless vessel is already on demurrage;
>
> (f) Intervention of Sanitary customs and /or other constituted authorities
>
> (h) Any other causes beyond control of the Charterers

Their argument was two pronged. First, they argued that sub-clause (h) gave them an all-weather defence when the delay was not caused due to their fault. Second, they argued that actions of the port authority fell within sub-clause (f). The latter argument was only made in the Court and was not canvassed before the arbitrator.

Analysis:

When a charterparty states specific clauses before the general clause, then the general clause takes color from the specific clauses.

The case of the charterer before the arbitrator had to be considered in totality. Before the arbitrator, the charterer had argued the cause and effect of the non-functioning crane as a composite bundle of facts. Their case essentially was that the port authorities had shifted the ship due to unsatisfactory performance of a crane. On a review of the facts, the arbitrator found that the ship had discharged more quantity than what was agreed in the charterparty. Thus, the arbitrator found that there was no question of under-performance. This finding of fact could not be challenged.

The charterer, however, argued that the arbitrator had ignored that the shipowner had admitted to the under-performance in the Statement of Facts (SoF). The shipowner had qualified the Statement by stating that the under-performance was 'alleged'. This could not be taken as an admission. The charterer had also not produced any other evidence to show that the port authorities had shifted the ship due to under-performance. Specifically, there was no material, communication, or port rules, to show that under-performance was the cause.

Finally, the charterer's attempt to move away from blaming the ship for under-performance, to the general exclusion clause (42, above) in the charterparty, also did not reap any benefit. The general exception clause was a common clause found in charterparties, the ambit and scope of which was widely understood. Sub-clause (h) was to be read along with the sub-clauses preceding it. Sub-clause (h) did not include the word 'whatsoever'. Therefore, the rule of *ejusdem generis*, 'of the same kind', applied to it. A reading of the preceding clauses showed that they did not give effect to the interplay of relations between the shipowner and charterer. They were about independent contingencies such as war, rebellion, lockouts, epidemics and accidents. The cause which leads to these contingencies did not arise out of any action between the parties. Even sub-clause (f) about the actions of constituted authority arose independent of the actions of the parties. The charterer had, by pleading its original case as that of under-performance, depended on the action of the shipowner. Therefore, they could not take refuge under sub-clause (h) either.

Arbitration, Incorporation Clause, Conduct

Title: United Shippers Limited *versus* Tata Power Company Limited

Citation: 2010 SCC Online Bom 2284

Court: High Court of Bombay

Issue:

This was a challenge to the appointment of an arbitrator on the basis that there was no subsisting arbitration agreement between the parties. The pertinent issue was whether a reference in subsequent agreements had incorporated the arbitration clause from the base contract.

Facts:

In 2003, the carrier and cargo interest entered into an agreement for transporting cargoes of coal from mother vessels to the onward rail carriage to Trombay Terminal Power Station. Thereafter in 2004, the parties again entered into a similar agreement with an identical arbitration clause. Thereafter, in 2005, the parties entered into a Memorandum of Understanding (MoU) for similar work but which had the following clause:

> The base contract to be used will remain the same as the contract for the period January 2004-2005, with modifications as necessitated from the above, and any other modification/corrections as mutually agreed.

Disputes in respect of demurrage, despatch, and payment, arose between the parties. The cargo interest argued that the above, incorporation clause, did not incorporate the arbitration clause from the base contract.

Analysis:

Parties had performed the obligations stated in the MoU. There was no doubt that the MoU constituted a valid, concluded and binding agreement between them.

The words of the incorporation clause were of wide import. The words 'base contract' indicated that the whole of the previous contract, as opposed to a part, had been incorporated into the MoU. The question of intention was also easily discernible in the fact that the three agreements were all in relation to identical work between the same parties, the only difference being the terms to which they attached. There was no evidence to show that the parties had chosen to exclude the arbitration clause, yet abide by all the other terms of the previous contract.

Additionally, the arbitration clause was not insensible, unintelligible or germane to the MoU. The cargo interest could not displace the effect of the fact that they were well aware of the arbitration clause of the previous agreements, by persuading the Court to rely on precedents which demanded clarity in the wording of an incorporation clause. Thus, the arbitration clause was incorporated into the MoU. The challenge was dismissed.

Demurrage, Failure to Load, Foreseeability

Title: William Henry Turner *versus* Kilburn and Co

Citation: 101 Ind Cas 854

Court: High Court of Calcutta

Issue:

This was an appeal from a single judge decision in favour of the charterer, denying their liability to pay demurrage. The issue was whether the charterer's failure to provide cargo made them liable for demurrage. The pertinent issue was whether there was anything in the charterparty which disallowed the shipowner from claiming.

Facts:

Sometime in 1920, the *SS Zingara* was chartered for two consecutive voyages from Calcutta, India, to Bombay, India. The cargo to be transported was coal, in bulk. In consequence of both voyages, the ship arrived at port, gave a notice of readiness to the charterer and the same was accepted by them on both occasions. However, the charterer was not ready to load the required cargo.

Before the single judge, the charterer argued that, at the time of negotiating the charterparty, the shipowner was made aware of certain facts, about difficulties that may arise in effecting shipment in time. Additionally, they argued that this eventuality should be read into the exception clause of the charterparty. This found favour with the single judge who held that the shipowner ought to have contemplated and did contemplate this kind of delay. As per the single judge, this was not an unreasonable delay and therefore, the charterer was not liable. The shipowner argued that the charterer was under an absolute obligation to supply cargo. This absolute obligation meant, that the charterer should have a cargo ready for being loaded into the vessel, on the expiration of 24 hours after notice of its arrival in port, at the place of loading, has been given.

Analysis:

The shipowner is responsible for getting the ship to the location specified in the charter party, and the charterer must prepare the cargo so that it may be loaded into the ship as soon as the vessel arrives at the location specified in the charter party.

The undisputed fact was that the charterer did not have a cargo of coal ready to be loaded into the ship. The charterparty did not state that the coal was to come from a particular colliery. Circumstances affecting supply from a particular place could have been considered in interpreting the charterer's obligation, if those circumstances were known to both parties. However, because the charterparty did not specify which place the cargo was to come from, the exception clause could not take effect in this case. Therefore, the charterer could not rely on the argument that the shipowner should have reasonably contemplated the delay.

It also did not help the charterer's case that the charterparty mentioned specific lay-days. The charterparty did not have an exception, of the kind argued by the charterer, to their obligation to load within this period.

Laytime, Weather Working Day, Meaning at Formation

Title: Steel Authority of India *versus* Western Bulk Carriers KS

Citation: [2010] OMP 401/2003

Court: High Court of Delhi

Issue:

This was a challenge by the charterer, to an arbitral award holding them liable for not discharging cargo on a weather working day, by considering that day in the laytime calculation. The issue before the Court was to assess the correct interpretation of the term 'weather working day'. The pertinent issue was whether a port notification, calling it a 'non weather working day', was to be taken as determinative of the right interpretation.

Facts:

In June 1995, the *MV Nand Swasti* was chartered to carry cargo to Vishakhapatnam, India. During discharge at Vishakhapatnam, the port authority issued a notification that one of the days was a 'non weather working day'. This was duly registered in the Statement of Facts (SoF) by the charterer. The shipowner's comment in response stated that laytime had to be counted as per the terms and conditions of the related charterparty. Crucially, the timesheet reflected that rain and weather delay lasted from 1000-1800 hours on this day. The charterparty clause relating to discharge stated, as follows:

Charterer's guarantee to discharge the cargo at the average rate of 5000 MT basis five or more hatches and pro rata for less number of hatches, per weather working day, Saturday afternoon, Sundays, charterparty holidays excepted, even if used unless the vessel is already on demurrage.

Analysis:

Terms of the charterparty have to be construed according to their plain and natural meaning that was understood by the parties to the contract at the time of formation of the charterparty.

It was clear that the discharge clause (above) mandated that the Charterer had to discharge 'per weather working day'. Judicial precedent had established that a weather working day is a day on 'which the weather permits the relevant work to be done'. The timesheet evidenced that the discharge was only prevented for 08 hours on the day, the remaining hours were not such as to prevent discharge.

The arbitral tribunal gave that meaning to the term which would be understood by commercial people. The tribunal noted that there were no judicial precedents in support of the argument that the port authority's notification was to be taken as determinative of the interpretation. The tribunal also noted that it was international practice to only exclude the time period during which discharge was actually interrupted or impossible. The tribunal also laid emphasis on the charterer's own statement that some of the vessels at the port may have been discharging. This showcased the true position that rain had not caused interruption or impossibility of discharge.

Consequently, the tribunal did not allow for this day to be taken out of the laytime calculation.

The Court agreed with the reasoning of the arbitral tribunal. It added, that if on a day it is possible to discharge, then it cannot be termed as a 'non weather working day'. It was telling that discharge was possible in the remaining 16 hours of the day. The relevance of the port notification depended on whether the charterparty gave it such a recognition but there was no reference in the charterparty to it. The port notification, thus, held no determinative value.

Laytime, Discharging Rate, Practicality

Title: The Union of India *versus* The Great Eastern Shipping Co Ltd

Date: 02nd December 2013

Court: High Court of Bombay

Issue:

This was an appeal from a single judge decision affirming three arbitral awards that favoured the shipowner's interpretation. The Court was faced with the issue of accepting the correct formula for calculating the rate of discharge out of two different interpretation. The pertinent issue was whether the heavy hatch formula, canvassed by the charterer, was acceptable for computing the rate.

Facts:

Through three different charterparty(s) in September-October 1988, the vessels *MV Jagdeesh, MV Jag Vivek,* and *MV Jag Vishnu,* were hired. They were all to carry similar cargo from Portland, Oregon, the United States of America, to Veraval, Karwal (nominated later), Vishakhapatnam, Haldia, and Kolkata, all in India. As is common, the three vessels either incurred demurrage or incurred dispatch. The rival contentions for calculating laytime turned on the interpretation of the following clause:

17. DISCHARGING RATE/TIME ETC.

(a) Cargo to be discharged by Consignees stevedores, free of risk and expense to vessel at the average rate of 1000 metric tons basis five or more available workable hatches and prorate for less number of hatches, per weather working day of 24 consecutive hours, Saturday afternoon, Sundays and charter party holidays excepted, even if used, always provided the vessel can deliver at this rate.

The charterer wanted that the above should be interpreted as meaning that each of the hatch should be discharging 200MT. Therefore, if any one hatch completes discharge then a consequent reduction in used laytime was to follow. The shipowner argued that the clause meant, that an overall rate of 1000MT had to be maintained with the qualifications that if a hatch was unavailable at the beginning, then the overall rate would be reduced *pro-rata* and, if a hatch became unworkable midst-discharge, then used laytime would be reduced. The arbitrators as well as the single judge sided with the shipowner.

Analysis:

A cargo ship is not only a transport, but it is also a warehouse where the operation to load and unload is carried out by a different party (charterer), and the warehouse operator (shipowner) is responsible for facilitating the process. The hatches fall within the facilitation function as they are parts of the ship. If the hatches do not function properly, they affect the charterer's ability to discharge. However, since the hatches are the responsibility of the shipowner, the liability, if any, emanating from this process is theirs. While if the charterer fails to discharge in time, they are liable to the shipowner for making the ship wait. Clauses like the present one attempts to provide a threshold for the two parties to be able to delegate responsibility and establish liability. By giving the interpretation that the charterer intended to give to this clause, the charterer can effectively reduce their exposure to liability by utilising one hatch over the other.

The concept employed in the charterer's argument is known as the 'heavy hatch formula'. The Court pointed out that one of the consequences of employing this formula is that the rate of 1000MT mentioned in the clause above would have to be wholly ignored. This seemed unreasonable and unrealistic because it presumes the availability of exactly the same amount of cargo in each hold. In other words, what the charterer was arguing for was a 'per hatch formula'. On this approach, the laytime would never be calculated with reference to the overall rate, 1000MT. However, that rate was the express mandate in the clause.

The reference to 'available workable hatches' in the clause was not meant to replace the overall rate but to provide a qualification as argued by the shipowner. This was what would have been understood by practical men undertaking the trade of shipping and cargo transportation. The clause seemed to provide primacy to the overall rate. It was also telling that the charterer was not able to prove how the heavy hatch formula would have made any difference to their liability. The charterer's argument was not accepted and the shipowner's interpretation, as accepted by the arbitral tribunal, was held to be correct.

Incorrect Shipping Mark, Bank Obligations, Unconditionality

Title: Centax (India) Ltd versus Vinmar Impex Inc.

Citation: AIR 1986 SC 1924

Court: Supreme Court of India

Issue:

This was an appeal from a High Court division bench order, preventing the buyer from restraining their bank from releasing funds to the shipowner promised under a letter of indemnity/ guarantee. The issue was whether the buyer could invoke such a restriction even though it had accepted delivery, sold the goods, and made a profit. The pertinent issue was whether the non-declaration or misdeclaration of the shipping mark affected the buyer adversely.

Facts:

Sometime in 1985, the buyer in India and the seller from Singapore entered into a contract for sale and transportation of High-Density Polythene Powder on CIF basis to Kolkata, India. One of the clauses required the seller to mention the shipping mark '5202' on the bills of lading. It was also agreed that the sale would be facilitated by letters of credit. Accordingly, the buyer's bank in India opened a letter of credit benefitting the seller. *MV Ganges Pioneer* brought the goods to Kolkata. However, the seller had not sent the original documents to the buyer and thus, the shipowner refused to deliver the goods to the buyer. On the seller's insistence, the buyer asked its bank to issue letters of indemnity/guarantee to the shipowner against which the goods would be delivered to the buyer. These were also signed by the buyer. After receiving the goods, the buyer sold the goods for a profit but did not pay the seller. When the shipowner demanded payment from the bank, the buyer filed a suit for breach of contract against the seller for sending inferior quality (grade) goods relatable to shipping mark 5502 and not 5202, for failing to send the shipping documents, and claiming damages. The buyer also made an application for restraining the bank from making payment to the shipowner. The application is pertinent to this note.

Analysis:

Shipping marks cannot be used to conclusively imply that the quality (grade) of the goods is inferior. The High Court was correct in noticing that the buyer had not showed any evidence that they suffered a loss due to this difference. Inversely, the buyer had actually made a substantial profit on the sale. This took away any prima facie strength from the buyer's argument. Thus, the balance of convenience lay in favour of allowing the payment from the bank to the shipowner.

Another problem in the buyer's case was that the letters of indemnity/guarantee, executed by the buyer's bank and countersigned by the buyer, had unconditional wording. There was past judicial precedent to establish that Courts should exercise extreme caution before interfering with irrevocable obligations assumed by banks as this could be detrimental to international commerce. Accordingly, a banker's letter of indemnity fell in the same grouping as a bank guarantee and a bank's letter of credit. The restriction demanded by the buyer could not be upheld and the bank was liable to make payment to the shipowner.

Laytime, Calculation, Evidence and Reasonability

Title: PEC Limited *versus* ADM Asia Pacific Trading Pte Ltd

Citation: 235 (2016) DLT 207

Court: High Court of Delhi

Issue:

This was an appeal by the buyer from an arbitral award that awarded demurrage payment in favour of the seller. The issue was whether calculation of laytime had been done according to the terms of the contract. The pertinent issue was whether the provisions for fumigation, minimum number of hatches, and strikes, were interpreted correctly to determine laytime and subsequent demurrage.

Facts:

In July 2008, the buyer entered into two contracts of sale for Canadian Yellow Peas with the seller on 'C&F Free Out' basis. The seller provisioned *MV Tu Qing* to bring the cargo from Vancouver, Canada, to Vishakhapatnam and Kolkata, India.

At the first port of discharge, Vishakhapatnam, the vessel arrived and provided a Notice of Readiness (NoR) to the buyer. The discharge duly commenced. However, fumigation of the cargo holds was completed two days later. As per the terms of the contract, fumigation was to be conducted prior to sailing. The buyer argued that this nullified the validity of the NoR.

Additionally at Vishakhapatnam, only three of the vessel's hatches were made available. At Kolkata, only two were made available. As per the terms of the contract, discharge was to be done on the basis of an average rate, based on minimum number of four hatches or pro rata. The buyer argued that this should have led to a pro rata increase in laytime.

Finally, the buyer argued that period of strikes due to political disturbance had to be seen as force majeure periods. The relevant clause of the contract named '..., any act of Govt., strikes or lockouts by workmen,...' as force majeure. It also stated that a certificate issued by the respective countries' Chamber of Commerce shall be sufficient proof of the event. The certificates provided for 'political disturbance'. However, the statement of facts (SoF) did not record any interruption due to strike.

Analysis:

The arbitral tribunal was correct in denying the buyer's argument about invalidation of the NoR due to lack of fumigation. A discharge certificate evidenced that discharge had begun before fumigation concluded. This was a self-destructive act and took away the strength of the buyer's argument. Furthermore, the terms of the contract did not provide for such a qualification to preface the NoR. The contract only stated that NoR was to be tendered WIBON (Whether In Berth Or Not), WIFPON (Whether In Free Pratique or not), and WIPON (Whether In Port Or Not).

On the argument of pro rata increase of laytime, the arbitral tribunal was correct to note that the buyer themselves had estimated a laytime of 10 days. Seen in the context of 40,000 MT loaded in 4 hatches, this could only signify that they were implicitly interpreting the effect of the clause as an overall rate, and not a per hatch rate. The arbitral tribunal's reliance on past judicial precedent that gave primacy to overall rate of discharge was justified. It was also significant that the clause provided for pro rata calculation of the discharge rate and not the allowed time. The buyer's method in which they had applied pro rata calculation of time was questionable. The buyer's argument was denied.

Finally, the arbitral tribunal's denial of the buyer's arguments of force majeure was also justified. The certificates provided by the buyer did not refer to any strikes during the discharge operations nor did the SoF record any interruption.

www.ingramcontent.com/pod-product-compliance
Lightning Source LLC
Chambersburg PA
CBHW020547030426
42337CB00013B/1001